Visit ✍ **W9-ANK-594**
www.FreeOhioFun.com

for
Free Ohio Fun
Free things to see and do in Ohio
for the whole family

updates, additions and in-depth articles

ISBN# 0-9724030-0-0

The book is divided into different subjects. Because of the nature of various venues, they could have been categorized in more than one section. In order to avoid redundancies, they were listed in the most relevant area of the book. Also, during the course of writing this book, a few venues began charging an admission fee. Therefore, they were omitted. And a couple of places have since closed.

As a precaution: Please call ahead to the venues you plan to visit to ensure that the hours, admittance and other data in this book have not changed. We assume no responsibility for omissions, inaccuracies or errors within the text of this book. However, we will take into consideration, any comments that would better represent the venues within, and add them to our Web site at www.freeohiofun.com.

Dedicated to
Rebecca, Cara and Dominic

i

ACKNOWLEDGEMENTS

I am thankful for having found a silver lining in being unemployed. It has enabled me to get to know my children, Cara and Dominic, in ways few fathers know their kids.

During the time my family spent together exploring Ohio for free, I have to thank the people at all of the places we visited for providing memorable experiences over the almighty dollar. And the people at our excellent government agencies such as the Ohio Historical Society and Convention and Visitors Bureaus at the state, county and local levels were very courteous and forthcoming in providing volumes of information - for free.

Most of all, my lovely wife Rebecca deserves my gratitude for being supportive of me in tolerance and encouragement while the chips were down.

This book is the result of a family's good times as they persevere through tough times.

CONTENTS

INTRODUCTION

Although many books have been written featuring travel and tourism highlights in Ohio, none focus on only those venues that offer FREE ADMISSION.

In an age when admission costs to a ballgame seem to double every five years, it has become increasingly important to budget for family entertainment. And believe me, it isn't only those with a "tight" budget looking for a bargain. Even those with lofty paychecks plan well and look for deals. It doesn't matter if the economy is in recession or experiencing unprecedented growth, people just don't ignore the word FREE.

Never mind the old myths such as "you get what you pay for" or "you don't get something for nothing." In this book, you will discover that it just isn't true. For example, the United States Air Force Museum in Dayton, Ohio is totally free and offers vast and extraordinary exhibits that rival the Smithsonian. And other museums that are admission-free weren't even built with tax dollars.

Okay, you're still not convinced and you figure out transportation and food costs. Well, if you want to be difficult, so can I. Technically, you can walk to the venue and eat a packed lunch of fruits and veggies homegrown from your garden by the seeds birds dropped on your patio while flying overhead.

Now, how significant can free admission be? Let's add it up. If you took the family out once every weekend and spent on average, $8.00 per person for admission to a venue, you would spend $1,164 per year for a family of four. However, if you alternated weekends with a "freebie" you would save half of that cost. Which, in turn, the money saved could buy all of the following:

- Four tickets to an Indians or Reds ballgame.
- Four tickets to Cedar Point, Kings Island or Six Flags.
- Dinner at a decent restaurant for an average size family four times over.
- Four movie tickets every month.
- And money left over for plenty of ice cream, putt-putt, videos and popcorn.

Regardless of the money you can save, you and your family can become rich with experiences as you discover a vast world of activities available for free - statewide. One may even go so far as to say that these freebies are, well - PRICELESS.

Satisfied? Okay, time to open your treasure chest and see what you get with your pass to **Free Ohio Fun**!

BIG WHEELS KEEP ON TURNIN'
(Aircraft, Autos, Boats, Rockets & Trains)

Nothing excites Americans more than "having wheels." Whether they're attached to their personal automobile or the bottom of a Space Shuttle, we love to move and see things move. Perhaps we move too much. But this would explain museums dedicated to our mobility.

Kids love train crossings but it's an adult who has an enormous model train museum. Some say women can't drive but they sure can fly as seen in the International Women's Air & Space Museum. Nobody you know may be work'n on the railroad but plenty of people across the state are working at train museums.

In this section, you will learn where to go to see everything from the Wright Brothers' Cycle Shop to outer space exhibits at the NASA Glenn Visitor Center.

Here's where the rubber hits the road! Whether it deals with a captain's wheel, train wheels, aircraft wheels or steering wheels, "big wheels keep on turnin'."

B & O RAILROAD MUSEUM AND
WILLARD AREA HISTORICAL SOCIETY
Admission is FREE

- Open Memorial Day - Call to set up an appointment between Memorial Day and Labor Day on Sundays from 1:00 p.m. - 4:00 p.m.
- Location: South Main Street · Willard, OH
- Phone: 419-935-0791

This local history museum features its railroad roots. It has a room primarily full of B&O railroad memorabilia. Kids will enjoy a restored caboose and its furnishings, as well as a box-car on display. In addition, a limited view of the train yard operation can be seen.

BLESSING OF THE FLEET
Admission is FREE

- When: Usually in April
- Location: Put-in-Bay, OH
- Phone: 419-285-2832
- Web Site: www.put-in-bay.com

Get ready for some fun on one of the Great Lakes as Lake Erie's summer hot spot kicks off another season with its Blessing of the Fleet. This annual celebration of the new fishing season includes a boat parade, music and entertainment.

Blessing of the Fleet celebrations also occur in Ashtabula, Ohio and other locations throughout the state's north coast and Ohio River communities.

DEPOT MUSEUM
Admission is FREE

- Open on Saturdays from 10:00 a.m. - 4:00 p.m.
- Location: 145 South Depot St. · Orrville, OH 44667
- Phone: 330-683-2426

This museum is operated by the Orrville Railroad Heritage Society and offers a plethora of railroad artifacts and memorabilia. The museum's collection is housed in a restored Railroad Union Depot. For a fee, actual train rides ranging from 50-120 miles are available.

DRESDEN JUNCTION
Admission is FREE

- Open Weekdays from 3:30 p.m. - undetermined. And Saturdays from 10:00 a.m. - 5:00 p.m.
- Location: 12585 Main St. · Trinway, OH 43842 (One mile north of Dresden, Ohio)
- Phone: 740-754-1290
- Web Site: www.geocities.com/dresdenjunction

Choo-choos from Lionel, Marx, Rail King, K-Line and MTH are on display here at this toy train & railroad artifacts museum. It features a 10X20 foot display of four running miniature trains. Other points of interest for model railroad enthusiasts may be the railroad artifacts dating back to the early nineteenth century through the early twentieth century. It's quite a personal collection for one man.

GOODYEAR WORLD OF RUBBER
Admission is FREE

- Open Mondays through Fridays from 8:00 a.m. - 4:30 p.m.

- Location: Goodyear's Corporate headquarters
  (Fourth floor of Goodyear Hall) · 1201 East Market St.
  · Akron, OH 44305
- Phone: 330-796-7117

This fascinating museum has more than just tires. It features displays depicting the history of blimps, the trucking industry, Indy racecars, a moon buggy and an artificial heart. It also exhibits a replica of a rubber plantation providing a hands-on experience, the history of the rubber industry and memorabilia. In addition, there is a reproduction of Charles Goodyear's workshop, including how he discovered the vulcanization process of rubber in his own kitchen.

GREAT LAKES MARINE AND
U.S. COAST GUARD MUSEUM
Admission is FREE

- Open Fridays, Saturdays and Sundays from Memorial Day through August from Noon - 6:00 p.m.
  (1:00 p.m. - 5:00 p.m. in September)
- Location: 1071 Walnut Blvd. · Ashtabula, OH 44004
- Phone: 440-964-6847

This museum is uniquely and appropriately housed in an 1898 lighthouse keeper's quarters and former residence of the Coast Guard Chief. It features various maritime models, paintings and marine artifacts. In addition, it displays shipping equipment, a restored pilothouse and the world's only working scale model of a Hulett ore unloading machine. Visitors also experience a grand view of the Ashtabula harbor, including tugboats and ore boats.

HARROD RAILROAD HERITAGE PARK & VETERANS' MEMORIAL PARK
Admission is FREE

- Open daily from dusk - dawn (Indoor artifacts can be seen by appointment)
- Location: Harrod, OH
- Phone: 419-648-3427

Have you ever wanted to show the kids the "man on the caboose" but discovered that trains today rarely have a caboose at all? Well, at this little "depot" you can see a renovated caboose, a 1905 Shay Engine, and a 100-year-old lumber office building. Inside, there are plenty of artifacts and memorabilia. The park also displays a full-size military U H-1 Huey Helicopter.

INTERNATIONAL WOMEN'S AIR AND SPACE MUSEUM
Admission is FREE

- Call for hours
- Location: Burke Lakefront Airport · 1501 North Marginal Rd. · Cleveland, OH 44114
- Phone: 216-623-1111
- Web Site: www.iwasm.org

This museum is dedicated to the historic accomplishments made by women pioneers of air and space travel. Some of the great women recognized at this museum include Sally Ride - the first American woman in space, Katharine Wright - sister of the Wright brothers, and Valentina Tereshkova - the first woman to orbit the Earth. In addition, there are many personal artifacts of great women pilots, as well as some personal memos by these women. News copy, magazines, and speech manuscripts are also displayed.

LAKE ERIE BOATING & FISHING FEST
Admission is FREE

- When: June
- Location: Cleveland's North Coast Harbor
  (Behind the Great Lakes Science Center and across
  from Voinovich Park)
- Web Site: www.boatohio.com/events/fishfest.shtml

This annual event is good for the entire family and includes
free fishing and casting clinics and much more. This thorough
hands-on introduction to boating and fishing life includes free
boat rides, tours of the U.S. Coast Guard cutter and a great
lakes steam ship, free vessel safety checks, entertainment,
fishing from boats and much more. It also marks Cleveland's
"Blessing of the Fleet."

LINCOLN PARK RAILWAY EXHIBIT
Admission is FREE

- Can be viewed anytime
- Location: East Elm Street in Lima, OH
- Phone: 419-222-9426

This outdoor display features the following, which are also
under lights after dark:

- The last steam engine built in Lima
  (Locomotive No. 779)
- 1883 luxury private car built for
  Chauncy DePew by Pullman
- 1882 Nickle-plated caboose
- and authentic 1895 Country Station by
  DT&I Railroad

MARITIME MUSEUM OF SANDUSKY
Admission is FREE

- Open May 1 - Labor Day from Tuesdays through Saturdays from 10:00 a.m. - 4:00 p.m. and Sundays from Noon - 4:00 p.m. From Labor Day - December 23rd, it is open Fridays, Saturdays and Sundays from Noon - 4:00 p.m. And from January 2nd - April 30, it is open on Saturdays and Sundays from Noon - 4:00 p.m.
- Location: 125 Meigs St. · Sandusky, OH 44807
- Phone: 419-624-0274
- Web Site: www.sanduskymaritime.org

This maritime museum reflects the history of the Sandusky, Ohio's region and its connection to the Lake Erie shipping industry, boating, fishing and more. Its many exhibits and collections depict the Sandusky Bay history and displays ship models and viewing of wooden boats being built. In addition, the museum hosts various events.

MEDINA TOY AND TRAIN MUSEUM
Admission is FREE

- Open Saturdays from 10:00 a.m. - 5:00 p.m. and Sundays from Noon - 5:00 p.m.
- Location: 7 Public Square · Medina, OH 44256
- Phone: 330-764-4455

All aboard! Make this a whistle-stop and see plenty of railroad memorabilia. The museum features running exhibits of model trains, interactive children's exhibits, real train exhibits, model cars and airplanes dating back to 1900, toys, dolls and more. In addition, there are more than 500 actual train engines on display and a library containing more than 500 books about trains that visitors may check out.

NASA GLENN VISITOR CENTER
Admission is FREE

- Open Mondays through Fridays from 9:00 a.m. - 4:00 p.m.; Saturdays from 10:00 a.m. - 3:00 p.m. and Sundays from 1:00 p.m. - 5:00 p.m. (Closed on major holidays)
- Location: 21000 Brookpark Road
  · Cleveland, OH 44135
- Phone: 216-433-2000
- Web Site: http://www.grc.nasa.gov/Doc/visitgrc.htm

You may think you have "the right stuff" but until you visit this museum/visitors center, you won't know for sure. The Center has eight galleries. A few of the featured galleries include Space Communications, John Glenn tribute and innovative engines of tomorrow. Other exhibits feature the Apollo Command Module used on Skylab 3, a space suit, moon rock, Microgravity Lab and Launch Control Center. It even has a baseball that was tossed around on a Space Shuttle Columbia flight.

Many special programs, events and presentations routinely take place at the NASA Visitors Center and in other Ohio communities. These include the Astromiles video presentation, live space shuttle broadcasts, zero gravity facility, wind tunnels, satellite control room, and Star Station One. The Star Station One Program shares the activities of the International Space Station with the public. Demonstrations are conducted the first Saturday of every month between 11:00 a.m. and 1:00 p.m. where audiences will see things like space food and clothing used.

THE WRIGHT "B" FLYER
Admission is FREE

- Open Tuesdays, Thursdays and Saturdays from 9:00 a.m. - 2:00 p.m.

- Location: 10550 Springsboro Park
  · Miamisburg, OH
- Phone: 937-885-2327

There's no charge for visitors to come see this aircraft in its hangar at Wright Brothers Airport. However, if you want a real ride in this flight-worthy replica of the first mass produced airplane designed by the Wright Brothers, it'll cost $125 per person. The plane was built by a group of aeronautical enthusiasts and can take short flights over the airport. The Wright Brothers plane in which this is designed after was used to correct problems in earlier flight-testing of the time.

U.S. AIR FORCE MUSEUM
Admission is FREE

- Open daily from 9:00 a.m. - 5:00 p.m.
  (Closed on major holidays)
- Location: Wright-Patterson Air Force Base in Dayton, OH
- Phone: 937-255-3286
- Web Site: www.wpafb.af.mil/museum/index.htm

Wow! This is more than a museum, it's an aviation time capsule and modern marvels all under one roof. It's no wonder this is the oldest and largest military aviation museum in the world. And it has more than 300 aircraft and missiles on display. More than 1.5 million people come from around the world to tour this museum, which includes aircraft galleries featuring the early years of flight and mid 20th century war planes to space flight and Presidential aircraft. That's right. Just about anything from the Wright Brothers to the Space Shuttle eras of flight can be seen in one place. Be sure to bring a camera and flash because the aircrafts are certainly picturesque as well as the realistic mannequins used in displays to depict authentic scenes. In addition, visitors are treated to a free documentary film in the auditorium on weekends. But that's not all. There are also thousands of aeronautical artifacts throughout, including military uniforms and flight jackets dating back to 1916 and personal items such as diaries, medals and more from the pilots who flew these man-made machines into the heavens above. Many displays are interactive and feature videos depicting detailed accounts of various moments in the history of flight. For a fee, there is also an IMAX theater and show open daily on the site. Attached to the museum is The National Aviation Hall-of-Fame in which pioneers of flight are inducted annually with a special ceremony. This hall of fame features interactive exhibits demonstrating the significance of scientific and historical contributions made to air and space evolution.

WRIGHT CYCLE COMPANY
Admission is FREE

- Open Mondays through Saturdays from 8:30 a.m. - 4:30 p.m. and Sundays from 11:00 a.m. - 4:30 p.m. (Closed Mondays and Tuesdays from September 3 - May 26)
- Location: 22 S. Williams St. · Dayton, OH 45407
- Phone: 937-225-7705

Visitors are free to see where two of the world's most famous inventors labored in their craft. Only one of the actual buildings where the Wright brothers worked is still standing at its original location and this is it. They had five different bicycle shops, this being the fourth. Now restored, the building was home to the Wright's bicycle business from 1895 - 1897. It is where they were when they became obsessed with flying. And from there, these men, self-trained in the science of aviation, went on to build the world's first power-driven, heavier than air machine capable of free, controlled and sustained flight.

SOUNDS LIKE A PARTY!
(Festivals & Events)

Being a northern state, Ohioans take advantage of good weather whenever they get it. This is especially evident between Memorial Day and Halloween - when most of the state's festivals and outdoor events occur. Of course there are exceptions like the wintertime Ice Festival in Medina.

This section features only the festivals and events that are admission free. And it proves that you don't have to spend money to have fun. For example, merely showing up for some of the states more unusual fests is all you need to do. How could you not have fun at an underwear-festival?

Ohioans find a reason to celebrate just about anything. Here are some types of fests and events highlighted in this section: All horse parade, buzzard day, sauerkraut, twins, wooly bears, pork rinds, kites, scarecrows, popcorn, ice, kites, mining, hot air balloons, wild turkeys, pretzels and much more.

AKRON CIVIC THEATER'S
FANTASTIC FRIDAYS
FREE performances

- When: The first Friday of the month from 11:30 a.m. - 1:00 p.m.
- Location: 182 South Main Street in downtown Akron, OH
- Phone: 330-253-2488 or 330-535-3179
- Web Site: www.akroncivic.com

The Akron Civic Theater has provided free performances in the past including, ballet excerpts from the Nutcracker show during the holidays, holiday shows, organ concerts and barber-shoppers.

The theater was built in 1929 by John Eberson, a famous theater architect. Its interior is designed after a Moorish castle featuring Mediterranean décor, medieval carvings, Italian sculpture and other European antiques. The auditorium resembles a night in a Moorish garden that includes clouds and stars drifting across the domed ceiling. The Civic is only one of five remaining atmospheric theaters in the country.

ALL HORSE PARADE
Admission is FREE

- When: September
- Location: Delaware, OH
- Phone: 740-362-3851 or 800-335-3247
- Web Site: www.delawarecountyfair.com/ horseparade2.htm

Okay, no horsing around, this parade kicks off the annual Delaware County Fair. Well over 500 horses participate and many pull vintage memorabilia from yesteryear such as a horse drawn milk wagon, sleigh, carriage, fire engine, mail coach and even a hearse. The horses come in all sizes, shapes, colors and breeds.

14

ASIAN FESTIVAL
Admission is FREE

- When: May
- Location: Columbus, OH (Franklin Park)
- Web Site: www.asian-festival.org

This festival is a major draw in central Ohio and attracts approximately 50,000 visitors of all backgrounds annually. Not only will guests learn about the cultures and traditions of people from China, Japan, India, Indonesia, Cambodia, Korea, Malaysia, Thailand, Philippines, Laos and Pakistan - to name about a dozen, it presents a very rich and fun experience. Activities are abundant. They include performing and visual arts shows, children's activities, cultural displays, martial arts demonstrations, and educational exhibitions.

BUCKEYE FLINT FESTIVAL
Admission is FREE

- When: September
- Location: Courthouse Square · Newark, OH
- Phone: 740-345-1282

Okay rock lovers, this one's for you (and we're not talk'n rock music). Ohio's gem stone is Flint rock. At this festival, you will walk away with more knowledge about Flint than you ever thought possible. The festivities include everything from displays, entertainment, crafts and "The Lottery" - just kidding...about "The Lottery."

BUCKEYE TREE FESTIVAL
Admission is FREE

- When: Second Sunday in September
- Location: Ye Olde Mill · 11324 State Route 13 · Utica, OH

- Phone: 800-589-5000
- Web Site: www.velvet-icecream.com/buckeye2.html

The festival is located in the Buckeye Tree Grove at Ye Olde Mill in Utica, Ohio. Celebrate Ohio's state tree and heritage as you find yourself in a flashback to the 1800s with horse-drawn wagons and all. Storytellers and costumed native Americans and frontiersman add to the flavor of the event. Also in attendance are buckeye wood carvers, old-time musicians and wool spinners and weavers. Visitors will not want to miss the ceremonial American Indian dancing and the liars & fibbers tall tale contest. Other attractions are the buckeye exhibits, historical displays, pioneer village, quilting bee, artists and craftsmen and much more.

BUCYRUS BRATWURST FESTIVAL
Admission is FREE

- When: Mid August
- Location: Downtown Bucyrus, OH
- Phone: 419-562-BRAT
- Web Site: www.bratfest.org

This festival packs in three days of family-fun and more than 27 tons of the finest sausage cooking over open pits. In 2001, Ohio Magazine voted the Bucyrus Bratwurst Festival the "Best Food Festival." The festival celebrates this small Ohio town's German heritage with more than just bratwurst. It has more than 100 more delicious foods made from local family recipes that have been handed down from generation to generation dating back to "the old country."

BUZZARD DAY
Admission is FREE

- When: The first Sunday after March 15th
- Location: Hinckley, OH near Hinckley Lake off of Bellus and State Roads

- Phone: 330-278-2066
- Web Site: www.hinckleytwp.org/buzzardday.html

See buzzards (turkey vultures) come home to roost in the rock cliffs and ledges in Hinckley. This annual celebration dates back to 1957 when 9,000 visitors flocked the township to see the return of the buzzards from their winter hiatus. The event includes an early bird hike; skits, songs and stories performed in tents or in fields, displays, crafts, photos, contests and additional hikes. Don't miss this right to spring and learn about the legend that surrounds Buzzard Day and why so many buzzards and people come out in March.

CAPITAL HOLIDAY LIGHTS
Admission is FREE

- When: December weekends
- Location: Ohio Statehouse in downtown Columbus
- Phone: 800-345-4386

Feel that holiday spirit in the warm heart of Ohio as the State Capitol building is set ablaze with lights, music and entertainment. This holiday light show comes with the lighting of the statehouse holiday tree and the Brightster. The Brightster is a seven-foot candle and mascot of the show. Don't miss the high-tech lighting affects, indoor family activities and nightly outdoor stage shows.

CARAMEL FESTIVAL
Admission is FREE

- When: Labor Day Weekend
- Location: Winchester, OH
- Phone: 937-695-0236

Yes, this festival has caramel galore and a whole lot more. There is a parade, live Nashville entertainment and a children's show. In addition, don't miss the culinary auction, baby contest, games, crafts and rides.

CHICKEN FEST
Admission is FREE

- When: September
- Location: Barberton, OH at Lake Anna Park
- Phone: 330-753-8471

If you're waiting to be invited to the next wedding just so you can do the Chicken Dance, come to Barberton, Ohio's Chicken Fest. This three day street festival features the "Chick-O-Lympics" and plenty of finger licking fun. Whether you want to dance to live band music or have the kids join in on some games, this fest has something for everyone. Most of all, it has lots of chicken.

CHRISTMAS IN THE VILLAGE
Admission is FREE

- When: First two weekends in December
- Location: Waynesville, OH
- Phone: 513-897-8855

This seasonal event is billed as a traditional Dickens holiday complete with Victorian street strollers, horse drawn carriages, carolers and live nativity scenes. Don't miss the evening luminary display as 1300 luminaries light up Main Street. The festivities also include Dickens characters, community Christmas tree and Tuba Christmas.

CITY ORCHESTRAS
Offering occasional free concerts

Cincinnati Symphony Orchestra
The Cleveland Orchestra

Columbus Symphony Orchestra
Dayton Philharmonic Orchestra
Toledo Symphony Orchestra

www.cincinnatipops.org/ (Cincinnati)
www.clevelandorch.com (Cleveland)
www.csobravo.org/ (Columbus)
www.daytonphilharmonic.com (Dayton)
www.toledosymphony.com/ (Toledo)

These renowned orchestras and others throughout the state sometimes perform smaller, free concerts at various locations in their respective greater metropolitan areas throughout the year. Keep an eye open for announcements in local newspapers or by periodically visiting the respective Web addresses listed above to find out when the next free event is being planned.

CLEVELAND INSTITUTE OF MUSIC
Most events are FREE

- When: Varies
- Location: 11021 East Blvd. · Cleveland, OH 44106
- Phone: 216-791-5000
- Web Site: www.cim.edu

The Cleveland Institute of Music is a leading international conservatory. The school's teachers and students collaborate and provide concerts for the community at its main building at Cleveland's University Circle. Visitors may see fully staged operas, enjoy special events for children and listen to the CIM Orchestra perform. Concerts are held weekly. And events also take place at the Institute's northeast Ohio branch locations in Shaker, Orange, Hudson and Fairview Park.

COLUMBUS ARTS FESTIVAL
Admission is FREE

- When: June
- Location: Columbus, OH (downtown riverfront)
- Phone: 614-224-2606
- Web Site: www.gcac.org/artsfest/

Sunshine Artist magazine named this "one of the best festivals in the country" in its September 2000 issue. More than 300 fine artists and crafts-persons ascend on this national art show annually. You can see their works in the Artist's Market. Children will enjoy the entertainment at the Youth Stage where there's numerous fun-filled activities. In addition, there are art activities for adults to enjoy, live music, community stage performances and a sand castle competition.

COLUMBUS FAMILY FUN FEST
Admission is FREE

- When: September
- Location: Riverfront Amphitheater in downtown Columbus
- Phone: 614-645-3332
- Web Site:http://www.musicintheair.org/ festivals/CFFFmain.html

Spend an interactive day with the family at the Family Fun Fest in Columbus. It has plenty to do all day long. Past events included painting, digging for dino bones, wall climbing and rides. Also, kids can discover the food groups in a nutritional expedition or visit the Sports Spot. Since the event is on the waterfront, nautical programs are included like navigation and rope making. Plus, visitors can gaze at the Tall Ships and more.

COLUMBUS JAZZ AND RIB FEST
Admission is FREE

- When: July
- Location: Columbus, OH (Downtown at Riverfront/Bicentennial Park)
- Phone: 614-225-6922

Go from hot ribs to cool jazz at this smoke'n summertime traditional event. It is definitely a popular attraction as 500-700 thousand people flock to the aroma of tasty sauce and the sound of tasty-tunes. Live music is provided by nationally known artists and headlining local performers.

CORN FESTIVAL
Admission is FREE

- When: August
- Location: North Ridgeville, OH
- Phone: 440-327-3737

Living in Ohio, everyone needs to go to at least one corn festival. Join the North Ridgeville community for three fun summer days and experience Amish-style corn. The festivities include a parade, live bands nightly, corn eating contest, car show, horseshoe tournament, rides, kids games, crafts and a midway.

DAYTON HOLIDAY FESTIVAL
Admission is FREE

- When: Weekend after Thanksgiving through the end of December
- Location: Downtown Dayton, OH
- Phone: 937-224-1518
- Web Site: www.downtown-dayton.com/dhf.html

This is one of the best holiday celebrations in the state. It is designed to celebrate all holidays of the season. The festival's founder, Virginia Kettering, began the tradition approximately 30 years ago with the intent to bring the spirit of the season to all, regardless of means. And today, it still offers most activities for free.

It begins with the "Grande Illumination" and fantastic entertainment. Then, visitors can celebrate "Holidays Around the World" and enjoy the festive "Holiday Street Fair." Families will want to see the "Children's Parade", "Distinguished Clown Corps" and Noontime Entertainment Programs. And if that weren't enough, there's the Historic Neighborhood Trolley Tours, weekend activities, "Lighting Up Downtown", "Tuba Christmas", "Dayton's Holiday Hunt" and Santaland Animated Window Displays.

EASTER EGG HUNT
AT YOUNG'S DAIRY FARM
Admission is FREE for this event

- When: Easter Sunday at 2:00 p.m.
- Location: 6880 Springfield-Xenia Road
  · Yellow Springs, OH 45387
- Phone: 937-325-0629
- Web Site: www.youngsdairy.com

Young's Dairy Farm celebrates Easter with its annual Easter Egg Hunt rain, snow or shine. Easter egg hunts are broken down into various age categories: 4 and younger, 5-7 years old and 8-10 years old. This tradition at Young's Dairy has been going on for approximately 20 years and boasts having more than 4,000 hard-boiled and dyed eggs for the hunt. It also presents Barnabe - the mascot - so bring a camera for pictures to remember.

Young's Dairy Farm is a working farm that is family-owned

and operated. They plan many events and activities for the whole family. Additional points of interest, for a fee, include; homemade ice cream, watching cows being milked, goat petting, two restaurants, bakery, gift shop, driving range, batting cages, miniature golf and more.

FAIRBORN SUMMER PARK SERIES
Admission is FREE

- When: Fridays (June and July)
- Location: Community Park East · Amphitheater · 691 E. Dayton-Yellow Springs Road · Fairborn, OH (Rain Location: Fairborn High School Auditorium · 900 E. Dayton-Yellow Springs Road)
- Phone: 937-754-3090
- Web Site: http://ci.fairborn.oh.us/city/fonf.html

These Free On Friday concerts feature big band to jazz and include jugglers and other entertainment. It is a pleasant way to end the work week and sit in the warmth of the evening sun and enjoy outdoor concerts and shows for free. Past performances included plays like John Henry by the Mad River Theater Works; pop, soul, R&B, gospel, doo-wop and jazz by the cappella group - Fourth Avenue; Pop Wagner - the singer, lasso twirler performing cowboy anthems. Also, the Juggernaut Jug Band complete with washboards, washtubs, kazoos, jugs and you name it. Contemporary music, beach party music and civic band performances also fill the air with fun sounds.

FALL FESTIVAL FAMILY FUN DAY
Admission is FREE

- When: October
- Location: Lake Erie Nature and Science Center in Bay Village, OH

- Phone: 440-871-2900
- Web Site: www.lensc.org

If you want to experience Halloween by decorating pumpkins, playing games and spending the day with your kids making crafts, go to the Lake Erie Nature and Science Center. Don't be surprised if staff members walk around and let visitors pet giant snakes, turtles and other local wildlife. Visitors can take a short stroll to the nearby Huntington Beach on the Lake Erie shore. The center has many other exhibits inside and outside for all to enjoy. The Center's planetarium has ongoing programs to provide a show laden with stars.

FALL FESTIVAL OF LEAVES
Admission is FREE
- When: Third weekend in October
- Location: Bainbridge, OH
- Phone: 740-702-7677 OR 800-413-4118

See the autumn colors in the hills and valleys of the village of Bainbridge. The community is open to all visitors for their annual festive event to celebrate the season. It hosts parades, pageants, flea markets and a midway with entertainment for all. In addition, there is a pedal tractor pull, arts and crafts, plus several self-guided scenic tours of the colorful landscape.

FEAST OF THE ASSUMPTION
Admission is FREE
- When: Mid August
- Location: Little Italy's Murray Hill neighborhood in Cleveland, OH
- Phone: 216-421-2995

Whether you're Italian or not, this festival is popular for all walks of life. There is a traditional religious processional through the ethnic neighborhood streets following a mass at the church. Crowds are enormous as it seems all of northeast Ohio ascends on this little Italian-American community making it "Big Italy" if only for a few days. There is plenty of music, dancing, artwork, rides, and yes, great food. The area definitely is filled with an "old-world" atmosphere. The four-day celebration draws crowds of more than 100,000 annually. How can that many people be wrong? If you're looking for old-world charm, culinary delight and beautiful cityscape, this is the place to see.

FEAST OF THE FLOWERING MOON
Admission is FREE

- When: May (Memorial Weekend)
- Location: Chillicothe, OH (downtown at Yoctangee Park)
- Phone: 800-413-4118

This three-day themed event features Native-American dancing and Pow Wow, village and mountain-men encampments depicting pioneer life in the 19th and daily entertainment. In addition, it displays arts and crafts, traditional entertainment, food and a variety of activities.

FESTIVAL LATINO
Admission is FREE

- When: June
- Location: Columbus, OH (downtown)
- Phone: 614-645-7995
- Web Site: www.musicintheair.org

Celebrate Latin culture to the music of Salsa, Mambo, Flamenco, Merengue and Conjunto by some of the finest national and international Latino artists. Presentations also include traditional ballroom dancing, and those brave enough can partake in a dance class to learn to Tango. Traditional Latin cuisines and festival fare are served, and a marketplace provides cultural pottery, jewelry, arts and crafts. In addition, hands-on children's workshops are offered.

FESTIVAL OF FISH
Admission is FREE

- When: June (Father's Day Weekend)
- Location: Vermillion, OH at Victory Park
- Phone: 440-967-4477

This festive event features a lighted boat parade on the river and a "Crazy Craft" boat race. Pull up a lawn chair and make a day of it riverside, and take in the sun and "crazy crafts." If you get hungry, treat yourself to a Walleye or Perch sandwich. Now doesn't that sound yummy? Oh, there's plenty of activities, entertainment and crafts too.

GRANVILLE HOT LICKS BLUES FEST
Admission is FREE

- When: September
- Location: Granville, OH (Downtown)
- Web Site: www.gfabluesfest.com

If you have a taste for the blues, The Granville Federation for the Appreciation of the Blues was formed for you. These local blues enthusiasts want to share their love of blues music with anyone who will listen. And listen you will, as well as dance and sing to the works of "living legends" and that of local talent.

GRAPE JAMBOREE
Admission is FREE

- When: Last full weekend in September
- Location: Geneva, OH
- Phone: 440-466-5262

Join thousands as they descend on this resort-community to celebrate the grape harvest with a traditional grape stomping contest and two parades. Visitors are encouraged to taste grapes freshly squeezed and other grape-products. Other treats include: street dancing, unique exhibits, grape culinary contest, arts and crafts, and other activities for the entire family to have fun.

GREAT LAKES WOODEN SAILBOAT REGATTA
FREE for spectators

- When: August
- Location Battery Park · 701 East Water St. · Sandusky, OH
- Phone: 440-871-8194 or 440-458-5254

If you like regattas, come and see this one. Beautiful wooden sailboats, both large and small, grace the waters of Lake Erie in this annual attraction. See them race for special awards in numerous boating categories. It is definitely one way to enjoy a late summer afternoon, especially if it is sunny. Don't forget to pack a picnic basket.

GREAT OUTDOOR UNDERWEAR FESTIVAL
Admission is FREE

- When: Second week in October
- Location: Piqua, OH

- Phone: 937-778-8300

Word has it that this truly popular and fun-packed festival has been discontinued but we'll include it since it may return. Piqua, Ohio used to be the "Underwear Capital of the World." However, the once 18 productive under garment factories have since left. In honor of their heritage, the community hosted the Great Outdoor Underwear Festival, which included wild events like the Long John Parade, Undy 500, Drop Seat Trot, Bed Races and a Boxer Ball. My goodness, how can an event like this not continue?

HARVEST HOEDOWN FESTIVAL
Admission is FREE

- When: First weekend in October
- Location: Bloomingburg, OH
- Phone: 740-437-7531

This "hoedown" packs in the fun with a parade, antique tractor show, dog show, and my goodness - a tobacco-spitting contest. It also hosts a Ma & Pa look-a-like contest, old-fashioned bonnet-making contest and baking contest. But that's not all. It also provides hayrides, kiddie tractor pulls, pony rides and more.

HOCKING FALL COLOR TOUR
Admission is FREE

- When: October
- Location: Conkle's Hollow State Nature Preserve in Hocking Hills State Park
- Phone: 614-385-4402
- Web Site: www.hockinghills.com

It's hard to believe a place like this is really in Ohio. Its spectacular topography sets it apart from anything else the state offers anytime of year. But in autumn, there is no other place to better enjoy the foliage of the season. The park has many attractions for nature-lovers, bird-watchers and others. Visitors enjoy the many hiking opportunities, wildlife viewing and scheduled festivities. Be sure to call and find out more about this year's Color Tour.

HOT AIR BALLOON FESTIVAL
Admission is FREE

- When: June
- Location: Coshocton County Fairgrounds
- Phone: 740-622-5411

Originally called the Coshocton Hot Air Balloon Race, its name changed to reflect the more encompassing events that occur at this festival. Balloonists from all over Ohio and Michigan come to show off their colorful aircrafts. Balloon launches are held at dawn and dusk. And a "night glow" of balloons occurs after dark. Balloonists take part in various events such as dropping markers, while in flight, in attempt to hit a target on the ground. Other activities include children's bicycle races, live music, rides and little league baseball tournaments.

ICE FESTIVAL
Admission is FREE

- When: Mid February
- Location: Medina, Ohio's public square
- Phone: 800-463-3462

Brrrrr. If you have "cabin fever" and want to spend some time outside in the middle of a northeast Ohio winter, you need to stop in the historic town square in Medina, Ohio for their annual Ice Festival. There, you will see a small downtown seemingly from a Norman Rockwell painting. Even more, you will see beautiful artwork made from ice as carvers compete in crafting ice sculptures. Don't worry, there are plenty of nice little shops to duck in and warm up a bit.

INDIAN FESTIVAL
Admission is FREE

- When: Last weekend in August
- Location: Powhatan Point, OH
- Phone: 740-795-4440

The Powhatan Indian Festival is an authentic Native-American event. It includes storytelling, traditional ceremonial dances, archery, authentic arts and crafts and a historical reen-actment. If you ever wanted to experience Native-American culture up-close, this is one stop you will want to make.

INTERNATIONAL FESTIVAL
Admission is FREE

- When: Last full weekend in June
- Location: Veterans Park in Lorain, OH
- Phone: 440-277-5244
- Web Site: www.loraininternational.com

More than 70 nationalities are represented at this worldly festival. Each culture is represented with authentic ethnic food to dazzle any palette. Visitors may work the food off to toe tapping music and dancing. A parade procession makes its way down Broadway in downtown Lorain and a Princess Reception and Pageant has ladies appear like princesses from around the globe. Additional activities abound through-out the town.

INTERNATIONAL MIGRATORY BIRD DAY
Admission is FREE

- When: May
- Location: Magee Marsh Wildlife Area in Oak Harbor, OH or Ottawa National Wildlife Refuge or Maumee Bay State Park's Nature Center
- Phone: 419-898-4070
- Web Site: http://www.bsbobird.org

Events are held throughout the state to celebrate the peak of the songbird migration. The Magee Marsh Wildlife Area in Oak Harbor tour includes bird banding demonstrations and other events.

INTERNATIONAL STREET FAIR
Admission is FREE

- When: Saturday in Mid May
- Location: Court Street in Athens, OH
- Phone: 740-593-4330

This annual celebration recognizes the diversity of lifestyles and cultures found around the world. The International Clubs from Ohio University work with other organizations to promote understanding of world customs and cultures. The celebration includes poetry readings, skits, dancing, music, cultural dress, art, and ethnic food (fee). This family-oriented event is embraced by both students and the community. Not only is it fun to attend but it is very educational as well. You will find more than 40 cultural displays. That's more than you will experience at Disney's Epcot Center.

KIDS FEST
Admission is FREE

- When: Third Saturday in June

- Location: Lincoln Park Commons in Kettering, OH
- Phone: 937-296-2587

Kids Fest is an annual favorite amongst the locals in the Miami Valley region. The festivities are designed for both kids and parents to participate. Activities range from face painting to hands-on crafts. And there are other treats like roving clowns and other costumed characters.

KIDSPEAK KIDSFEST
Admission is FREE

- When: Third Sunday in September
- Location: Franklin Park , 1777 East Broad Street in Columbus, OH
- Phone: 614-645-3343

This annual festivity is a one-day celebration that includes everything from roving street performers, costumed characters and musical entertainment to fishing instruction, canoeing and hayrides. It also offers visitors a chance to create hands-on crafts and play games. Nonprofit youth service agencies from Central Ohio have many exhibits with information and free-bies for the taking.

KITE FESTIVAL
Admission is FREE

- When: Labor Day Weekend
- Location: U.S. Air Force Museum at Wright-Patterson Air Force Base in Dayton
- Phone: 937-255-3286
- Web Site: http://www.wpafb.af.mil/museum/

See the skies filled with kites at the annual two and a half day Kite Festival. Not only can you fly your kite with many others but you may also see demonstrations, workshops and competitions, and visit the world's oldest and largest aviation museum. Additional activities include a radio-controlled model aircraft event and other workshops like Kite Shoot Outs and more.

KWANZAA FESTIVAL
Admission is FREE

- When: 6:30 p.m. nightly from December 26 - January 1
- Location: Kanisa House II in Elyria, OH
- Phone: 440-366-5656

Celebrate African-American people, culture and heritage at this annual event. Kwanzaa is a weeklong celebration where family and friends gather to reflect on the seven principles of Kwanzaa. In short, it is a celebration of life for African-Americans beginning December 26th and lasting for 7 days. It is to honor the past, evaluate the present and dedicate to a fuller and more productive future. The seven principles are Unity, Self Determination, Collective Work and Responsibility, Cooperative Economics, Purpose, Creativity, Faith.

LAGRANGE STREET POLISH FESTIVAL
Admission is FREE

- When: The first weekend after the 4th of July
- Location: LaGrange Street between Central and Mettler Streets in Toledo
- Phone: 419-255-8406

See a city street transform into an authentic ethnic festival celebrating its Polish community's culture and traditions. Polka dancing and music are provided. In addition, there are plenty of children's activities, rides, crafts, polka contest and plenty of ethnic food.

LEBANON CHRISTMAS FESTIVAL
Admission is FREE

- When: First Sunday in December
- Location: Lebanon, OH
- Phone: 513-932-1100

Visitors definitely experience the holiday spirit when they visit this picturesque small historic Ohio town in December. The event features a candlelit parade of 60 vintage horse-drawn carriages. In addition, the streets are filled with strolling musicians and holiday characters. And a train display and more await those who come. Just the site of this small town lit up for the holidays is worth the trip.

MELON FESTIVAL
Admission is FREE

- When: Labor Day Weekend.
- Location: Village Square on State Route 113 East in Milan, OH.
- Phone: 419-668-5231

Where else can you see things like the Big Wheelie Race, Melon Eating Contest, kiddie pedal-tractor pulls and a two hour grand parade? The Melon Festival in Milan provides that and bands, a fireman's chicken barbecue, arts and crafts, antique car show and Queen's Contest. Oh, and plenty of melon in all shapes, sizes and forms. This three-day event packs in more than 100,000 visitors.

MINING AND MANUFACTURING FESTIVAL
Admission is FREE

- When: September
- Location: Cadiz, OH
- Web Site: www.harrisoncountyohio.org

Have you ever been to a coal-shoveling contest? Have you ever shoveled coal? Well, here's your chance. Swing over to Cadiz in September and watch people compete as they participate in a coal-shoveling contest. The festival also has a parade, a coalhouse, coal products, labor force bands and ethnic food. Grab your shovel and go.

MUSIC IN THE AIR
Admission is FREE

- When: Memorial Day through Labor Day
- Location: Various locations in Columbus, OH
- Phone: 614-645-7995
- Web site: www.musicintheair.org

More than 100 FREE outdoor performances featuring a variety of music, drama, dance and children's programs are arranged by the Columbus Recreation and Parks Department every year between Memorial Day and Labor Day. Locations and days of the week vary from event to event. Past Music in the Air events have featured gospel, folk and jazz music; music, dance, theater and interactive programs for kids; popular and classical music at Topiary Gardens; poetry, dance, "musical mornings" and much more. Plan to bring a blanket and picnic basket wherever you go to listen to the Music in the Air.

OHIO BALLET SUMMER FESTIVAL
Admission is FREE

- When: Various dates throughout the Summer
- Location: Various locations throughout greater Akron, OH
- Phone: 330-972-7900 or 216-661-6645
- Web Site: www.ohioballet.com

For more than 30 years, the Ohio Ballet has opened its season with a series of FREE outdoor shows. In recent years, more than 10,000 people turn out at approximately three locations to see eight performances in casual and family-friendly atmospheres. There are also interactive pre-shows for children before events where some kids are invited on stage to learn basic ballet moves and more.

OHIO HONEY FESTIVAL
Admission is FREE

- When: September
- Location: Courthouse Square in Oxford, OH
- Phone: 888-53-HONEY

Although not the feature attraction at this event, it is one of the most interesting at any event. See the Living Bee Beard as a trained professional allows a queen bee to be strapped to his chin and attract more than 15,000 additional bees to his face creating a bee beard. But that's not all, you can volunteer to kiss the man if you want - bee beard and all. Other events include a parade, face painting, magic shows, music, bee displays, classic car show, carnival rides, arts, crafts and entertainment.

OHIO PUMPKIN FESTIVAL
Admission is FREE

- When: The last full weekend in September
- Location: Barnesville, OH
- Web Site: www.pumpkinfestival.8k.com

This festival has many interesting activities taking place. Its contests include hog calling, pumpkin rolling, largest pumpkin, pumpkin pie eating and banjo and fiddle contests. If that weren't enough, there is a Giant Pumpkin Parade, tall tales, antique car show, quilts, crafts, farm machinery, music, food and entertainment.

OHIO RIVER STERNWHEEL FESTIVAL
Admission is FREE
- When: The weekend after Labor Day in September
- Location: Ohio River Levee at Front and Greene Streets in Marietta, OH
- Phone: 800-288-2577

Come to the River Sternwheel Festival and you will see Sternwheel boat races, fireworks and more than 30 stern wheelers docked for a weekend of fun. Music is continuous and national entertainers and local performers dazzle crowds. The event also has a car show, pageants, singing and dancing to country, rock and jazz musical performances. Visitors will also want to tour the historic river town of Marietta to take in the atmosphere and community.

OHIO SWISS FESTIVAL
Admission is FREE
- When: The last Friday and Saturday in September
- Location: Sugarcreek, OH
- Phone: 330-852-4113

Experience the best of Switzerland here in the "Little Switzerland of Ohio." Visitors will be drawn to the Swiss music and authentic Swiss costumes. There are tons of Swiss cheese to go around, polka bands, alpine horn players and a parade. On a more interesting note, come see the Steinstossen contest and see stone throwers compete or see Schwingfest - Swiss wrestling.

OPEN DART TOURNAMENT
Admission is FREE

- When: First weekend in May
- Location: Various locations in Ross County - Chillicothe, OH
- Phone: 740-702-7677 or 800-413-4118

If you are a dart enthusiast or would just find entertainment in watching professional dart-throwers from across the country compete, you may want to attend this annual tournament. The contest's winners receive prizes and trophies.

PIONEER DAYS
Admission is FREE

- When: First Weekend in August
- Location: 352 Cherry Street · Gnadenhutten, OH Historical Park and Museum
- Phone: 614-254-4143

Celebrate pioneer-style at Gnadenhutten Historical Park & Museum. Visitors will see a parade and a mixture of other entertainment. There is an 1840s pioneer encampment sure to make children and adults alike appreciate their modern amenities. In addition, there are plenty of arts, crafts and more to see at this traditional annual event.

PLANES, TRAINS AND AUTOMOBILES FESTIVAL
Admission is FREE on Saturday of fest Only

- When: June
- Location: 1080 Navajo Drive · Bluffton, OH (Bluffton airport)
- Phone: 419-358-5675

Kids will enjoy seeing people fall from the sky - via parachutes of course. Otherwise, that would just be sick. There are also plenty of antique automobiles and classic cars to see and model train displays too.

POPCORN FESTIVAL (MARION)
Admission is FREE

- When: Weekend after Labor Day
- Location: Marion, OH
- Phone: 740-387-FEST
- Web Site: www.popcornfestival.com

There's a lot to pop about at the annual Marion Popcorn Festival. For starters, it's claimed to be the largest popcorn festival in the world and attracts more than 250,000 visitors per year. With all of that notoriety, it's no wonder that the American Bus Association named it one of the Top 100 Events in North America. The free entertainment has included headlining bands like REO Speedwagon, Gloria Estefan, Huey Lewis and The Neville Brothers. In addition, the fest hosts a parade, bike tour, 5k run, fine arts and crafts, the Kiddie Korner and more than 50 softball tournaments. There are numerous rides and activities for the whole family, and of course, a popcorn museum, which displays The Dunbar Concession Wagon used by Paul Newman in Central Park to promote "his" popcorn and much more. Oh, and for art lovers, don't miss out on the popcorn sculptures.

POPCORN FESTIVAL (BEAVERCREEK)
Admission is FREE

- When: The weekend after Labor Day in September
- Location: Beavercreek, OH
- Phone: 937-427-5514
- Web Site: http://beavercreek.hcst.net/popcorn/

Hop on over to Beavercreek and see what's poppin'. This event was one of the Top-100 Events in North America, by the American Bus Association. With it come popcorn sculpture, popcorn showers and other popcorn specialties. It also features a 300 + unit parade and national recognized entertainment and balloon rally.

PORK RIND HERITAGE FESTIVAL
Admission is FREE

- When: June
- Location: Harrod, OH
- Phone: 419-648-3427
- Web Site: http://www.rudolphfoods.com/
  pork_rind_heritage_festival.htm

Rudolph Foods Company and Harrod, Ohio offer the Pork Rind Heritage Festival annually. Yes, Pork Rind Festival! If you want to see how many tasty ways you can prepare a pork rind, eat fresh popped pork rinds or enjoy a hog roast, this festival is for you. It also features a parade, live entertainment and crafts.

PREBLE COUNTY PORK FESTIVAL
Admission is FREE

· When: Third full weekend in September
· Location: Preble County Fairgrounds in Eaton, OH
· Phone: 937-456-7273
· Web Site: www.porkfestival.org

This festival comes complete with a butchering and sausage making demonstration. If that sounds a bit too gruesome for you, go see the magic show, parade, contests and other entertainment planned. Visitors can learn new ways to prepare pork, see the new litter of piglets or enjoy a variety of live music and see the pig races. No matter what you choose to do, you will find this to be more than your ordinary festival.

PRETZEL FESTIVAL
Admission is FREE

- When: September
- Location: Germantown, OH
- Phone: 937-855-4687

Since President George W. Bush had a scare with a pretzel one evening in the White House, Germantown, Ohio sent an open invitation for the President to attend its Pretzel Festival. Please note, there is no guarantee you will see the President of the United States should you attend this festival. However, you will enjoy a good pretzel, live music and shows, rides, games, food and crafts.

PUMPKIN FESTIVAL (CIRCLEVILLE)
Admission is FREE

- When: October
- Location: Circleville, OH
- Phone: 740-474-7000
- Web Site: www.pumpkinshow.com

Great pumpkins Charlie Brown, this is said to be Ohio's oldest and largest pumpkin celebration. It hosts seven different parades in half as many days. This includes the Pumpkin Parade, Pet Parade and Baby Parade to name a few. The events also include a Big Wheel Race, world's largest pumpkin pie, a pumpkin toss, pie eating competition and Fun Show. Additional contests of interest include hog calling, egg toss and pumpkin carving. Many displays, arts, crafts and live entertainment also accompany the festivities as well as plenty of pumpkins, squash and gourds.

RIVER DAYS
Admission is FREE

- When: Labor Day Weekend
- Location: Portsmouth, OH
- Phone: 740-355-6622 or 740-354-6089

River Days is an annual family-oriented event that features a parade, arts and crafts, rides, entertainment, events, queen's pageant and a whole lot more.

RIVERFEST
Admission is FREE

- When: Labor Day Weekend
- Location: Promenade Park in Toledo, OH
- Phone: 419-243-8024
- Web Site: www.citifest.org/riverfest

Head for downtown Toledo to send summer off in style. Riverfest is a three-day event that attracts more than 125,000 visitors to the shores of the Maumee River to have fun. The festival features a variety of musical entertainment from nationally known bands to local favorites. Many hands-on kid's activities are available as well as interactive games. A spectacular fireworks display set to music is an annual favorite. Fairly new attractions include the "Holy Toledo, Let's Jam" day of Christian music and SkateFest, which determines the top boarders in the region as they navigate through obstacles. Other points of interest include the Teen stage where teen bands play to the audience and a progressive art display of a 40-foot long graffiti mural.

SAUERKRAUT FESTIVAL
Admission is FREE

- When: Second full weekend in October

- Location: Waynesville, OH
- Phone: 513-897-8855

The people of Waynesville may debate whether they are the Antiques Capital of the Midwest or the Home of the Sauerkraut Festival but make no mistake they have lots of both. Some say antiques and sauerkraut saved this little town. Either way, more than 11,000 pounds of sauerkraut are cooked up for the annual festival. Some of the more unique recipes for visitors' indulgence include sauerkraut ice cream, brownies, doughnuts and pizza. The local folks urge that just because it's made with sauerkraut doesn't mean it tastes like it. Awards are given to those with the largest cabbage, greenest cabbage and the most "congenial" cabbage. Featured attractions are the antique car parade, arts and crafts show, German bands and folk dancers, entertainment and good old-fashioned spelling-Bee contests.

SCARECROW FESTIVAL
Admission is FREE
- When: Mid September
- Location: Washington Court House, OH
- Phone: 740-636-2340

The Scarecrow Festival is fitting in Ohio. This street fair has a parade, live entertainment and a living scarecrow contest.

SHAKESPEARE FESTIVAL
Admission is FREE
- When: 6:30 p.m. Fridays through Sundays in June and July
- Location: The season is split between two locations in northeast Ohio. Shaker Heights Colonnade at 3450 Lee Road in Shaker Heights, OH and Tri-C West Campus at 11000 Pleasant Valley Road in Parma, OH

43

- Phone: 216-732-3311
- Web Site: www.cleveshakes.org

Come early to find a good lawn seat and bring a blanket for the whole family. This award winning show has been running for several years and has wowed thousands. Visitors will enjoy Shakespeare the way Shakespeare was meant to be enjoyed - amidst the festive atmosphere of a vibrant community. The actors and staff offer a show that is fresh and entertaining for the modern world. So, enjoy good old-fashioned theatre in the glow of the summer's afternoon sun.

SHAKESPEARE IN THE PARK
Admission is FREE

- When: Summers
- Location: Southside of Schiller Park in the historic German Village in Columbus, OH
- Phone: 614-444-6888
- Web Site: www.theactorstheatre.org

These free performances in the park began more than 20 years ago. It is said that the tradition started when a dog led cofounders Patricia and Gary Ellson there. Once there, they found an unused band shell. Having a love for Shakespeare, the two sought permission to use the stage to offer free shows to the community. Well, as they say, the rest is history. What was started as an amateur group grew into a professional production and has attracted hundreds of thousands of spectators. Enjoy this fascinating tradition. Note, you may want to call first to see if your dog is allowed to attend.

STRAWBERRY FESTIVAL
Admission is FREE

- When: June
- Location: Troy, OH

- Phone: 800-348-8993

Although there are other strawberry festivals in Ohio and some that offer free admission, the Troy Strawberry Festival is one of the best. Troy is proclaimed by locals to be the Strawberry Capital of Ohio. The festival attracts more than 250,000 visitors. Its featured attractions include a parade, bed races, hot air balloon rally, car show, arts and crafts, sporting events and children's events. Also, there are hovercraft and raft races on the river. In addition, there are pie-eating contests, kiddie tractor-pulls, tug-of-war, rubber duck race, Berry Special Olympics, Big Wheel Races and a myriad of other activities.

SWEET CORN FESTIVAL
Admission is FREE

- When: August
- Location: Community Park East on Dayton-Yellow Springs Road in Fairborn, OH
- Phone: 937-878-7040

I can't resist…this is an EAR-Resistible festival. You've seen eating contests of all sorts but until you've seen teeth chop away at corn-on-the-cob like an old-fashioned typewriter, you aint seen a corn-eating contest. There's also a variety of entertainment, activities, arts and crafts and lots of fresh corn.

THUNDER IN THE HILLS
HYDROPLANE RACE
Admission is FREE

- When: September
- Location: Rocky Fork State Park in Hillsboro, OH
- Phone: 937-393-4284

If you like boat races, come and see "the largest hydroplane boat race in the country." And while you're there, you may want to participate in other festive activities, entertainment and a 5k run and health walk.

TUSCARAWAS COUNTY
ITALIAN-AMERICAN FESTIVAL
Admission is FREE

- When: August
- Location: New Philadelphia, OH
- Phone: 330-343-1272

Celebrate Italian-American heritage with plenty of food, music, dancing and fun. This festival features Bocce and Morra tournaments, a pizza eating contest, spaghetti sauce contest, amateur wine makers contest and plenty of other activities for the family. An outdoor mass is also held on the town square.

TWINS DAY FESTIVAL
FREE for TWINS ONLY

- When: The first full weekend in August
- Location: Twinsburg, OH
- Phone: 330-425-3652

If you want to see double - attend the next Twins Day Festival in Twinsburg, Ohio. If you and a twin go, your admission is FREE. This is said to be the largest gathering of twins in the world. And it's right here in Ohio. Officials estimate that more than 2,500 sets of twins appear every year. Now that's quiet a sight. Twins from around the world participate in a parade appropriately named the Double-take Parade, which has been nationally televised. Other activities include entertainment, fireworks and contests.

VELVET ICE CREAM FESTIVAL
Admission is FREE

- When: May
- Location: Ye Olde Mill · 11324 State Route 13 · Utica, OH
- Phone: 800-589-5000
- Web Site: http://www.velvet-icecream.com/icecreamfestival2.html

What's summer without ice cream. If you like ice cream, you will love this festival, which has plenty of that and more. It includes a magic circus, arts and crafts exhibits, custom/classic cars and rod run, sheep herding with Border collies, ice cream eating contests, entertainment and antique gas engines.

WILD TURKEY FESTIVAL
Admission is FREE

- When: May
- Location: McArthur, OH
- Phone: 740-596-4945

Some festivals have the expected contests, some have a few that are interesting and only a hand-full have the truly unique. At the Wild Turkey Festival in Vinton County, you will hear people making the strangest noises while they compete in the Turkey Calling Contest. This street fair features a parade, car show, quilt show, rides, games, arts and crafts, and plenty of entertainment.

WOOLY BEAR FESTIVAL
Admission is FREE

- When: The first Sunday in October
- Location: Vermilion, OH

- Phone: 440-967-4477

Everyone knows about Ground Hog Day but a fuzzy little critter in Vermilion will forecast how severe of a winter Ohio can expect before it even starts - or so they say. The Wooly Bear is a fuzzy caterpillar. It is said that if the black band on the critters brown back is wide, get ready for lots of white stuff to fall from the sky. Well, this festival pays tribute to the Wooly Bear with its annual weather forecast, parade, wooly bear races and many contests, arts and crafts and additional entertainment for the whole family.

ZUCCHINI FESTIVAL
Admission is FREE

- When: August (The weekend prior to Labor Day)
- Location: Obetz, OH
- Phone: 614-497-2518

Come and get all the fresh zucchini you need to make bread and other treats to freeze for the winter. The Obetz Zucchini Festival has zucchini in the form of many different foods, including burgers and fudge. The event also hosts a parade and queens pageant, contests, arts and crafts, games and rides along the midway. Plus, a variety of music will fill the air along with the wonderful aroma of zucchini.

GREEN THUMBS & WET PALLETS
(Gardens & Art Museums)

It doesn't take a gardener to appreciate beautiful plant life. Ohio has many botanical gardens, arboretums, conservatories and horticultural centers open to the public. Many are free to visit.

For the artist in all of us, there are also museums of art, galleries, centers for the arts and other art centers waiting to please our pallets - for free.

Enter the world of gardens and art to test your green thumb or wet your pallet.

AKRON ART MUSEUM
Admission to the museum is FREE

- Please note that if you drive your own vehicle to the museum, there is a $2 parking fee for non-members (Waived for museum members)
- Open daily from 11:00 a.m. - 5:00 p.m.
- Location: 70 East Market Street · Akron, OH 44308-2084
- Phone: 330-376-9185
- Web Site: www.akronartmuseum.org

The Akron Art Museum enriches lives through modern art. Since being founded in 1922, in the basement of the Akron Public Library, the museum has become the leading museum of modern art in northeast Ohio. It's now located in a turn-of-the-century, award winning building that once served as the city's main post office.

In addition to its own collection, the museum features borrowed works showcasing a new temporary collection every 13 weeks. Past exhibits included pieces from the Smithsonian Institution, Georgia O'Keefe and Andy Warhol.

ALLEN MEMORIAL ART MUSEUM
Admission to the museum is FREE

- Open Tuesdays through Saturdays from 10:00 a.m. - 5:00 p.m. and Sundays from 1:00 p.m. - 5:00 p.m. It is closed on Sundays and major holidays.
- Location: Oberlin College · 87 North Main Street · Oberlin, OH 44074
- Phone: 440-775-8665
- Web Site: www.oberlin.edu/allenart

The Allen Memorial Art Museum was founded in 1917. Today, it's ranked among the finest college and university collections in the U.S. The collection contains more than 11,000 works of art that span history.

The buildings that house the art museum are eclectic architectural beauties. Part of the complex was built in 1917. It was designed by Cass Gilbert, and represents Tuscan Renaissance and Midwestern Vernacular architectural styles. The 1977 addition was designed in Orthodox Modernist style by Venturi, Scott Brown, and Associates.

The museum offers Tuesday Teas (for Free) on the second Tuesday of each month. Join the company of others (no registration required) and learn more about the collection. Talks begin at 2:30 p.m.

BUTLER INSTITUTE OF AMERICAN ART
Admission is FREE

- Open Tuesdays, Thursdays, Fridays and Saturdays from 11:00 a.m. - 4:00 p.m. and Wednesdays from 11:00 a.m. - 8:00 p.m. and Sundays from Noon - 4:00 p.m.
- Location: 524 Wick Avenue · Youngstown, OH 44502
- Phone: 330-743-1711
- Web Site: www.butlerart.com

Exhibitions include: Gary Bukovnik, A Ceramic Continuum, Don Gummer and Ben Schonzeit: Sculptural Glass Exhibition.

The Beecher Center is the south wing of The Butler Institute of American Art and includes exhibitions by Carol Adams, Patrick Boyd, Dennis Marsico, Bill Viola, Bill Thompson and Nam June Paik.

The Wean Archive Center/Hopper Library houses The Butler Library of art books and has searchable databases of archive material

Salem Branch

- Open Wednesdays through Saturdays from 11:00 a.m. - 4:00 p.m.
- Location: 343 East State Street · Salem, OH 44460
- Phone: 330-332-8213

This facility was designed by architect Robert Buchanan and is housed in a refurbished historic building on the city's main street. The Butler Salem offers four galleries: Salem Area Artists Guild, Edwin Shuttleworth, Ohio Contemporary Quilts and Margaret Lefranc. It also has temporary exhibitions from accomplished regional artists, works from prominent American artists and from the Butler permanent collection.

Trumbull Branch

- Open Wednesdays through Sundays from 11:00 a.m. - 4:00 p.m.
- Location: 9350 East Market Street · Howland, OH 44484
- Phone: 330-609-9900

CANTON MUSEUM OF ART
Admission is FREE ONLY on Tuesdays

- Open Tuesdays through Saturdays from 10:00 a.m. - 5:00 p.m. and Tuesday through Thursday evening hours are from 7:00 p.m. - 9:00 p.m. Sunday hours are 1:00 p.m. - 5:00 p.m.
- Location: 1001 N. Market Avenue · Canton, OH 44702
- Phone: 330-453-7666
- Web Site: www.cantonart.org

The Canton Museum of Art has fine art exhibits in its permanent collection as well as many traveling pieces appearing in the museum's galleries. Some past exhibits featured include

Bart Walter's Soul of Africa, The Road Less Traveled, Samuel Bak's Surrealism, The Potters of Mata Ortiz - Transforming a Tradition and Visions into The 21st Century - The New Age of Holography. In addition, the museum hosts many special events and classes.

CHADWICK ARBORETUM
Admission is FREE

- Open: Call for hours
- Location: Ohio State University · Columbus, OH
- Phone: 614-292-OHIO
- Web Site: http://chadwickarboretum.osu.edu/

This arboretum is funded by Ohio State University and serves as an outdoor laboratory. As such, it seeks to maintain an environment for teaching and research while building a relationship with the community and conducting academic initiatives.

The garden collections are categorized according to the following themes: Wildflowers, Hostas, Conifers, Annuals, Perennials, Native Trees, Roses and Willows. It also has a Learning Garden with three areas: A Landscape Room featuring urban garden themes and techniques, Named gardens recognizing donors with interesting plant collections and Trial Gardens for the purposes of research and demonstrations.

CINCINNATI ART MUSEUM
Admission is FREE on Saturdays ONLY. For those who are 17-years-old or younger, it is always FREE

- Open Saturdays from 10:00 a.m. - 5:00 p.m; Tuesdays, Thursdays and Fridays from 11:00 a.m. - 5:00 p.m; Wednesdays from 11:00 a.m. - 9:00 p.m. and Sundays from Noon - 6:00 p.m. Closed on Mondays, Fourth of July, Thanksgiving and Christmas.

- Location: 953 Eden Park Drive · Cincinnati, OH 45202
- Phone: 513-639-2995
- Web Site: www.cincinnatiartmuseum.com
- Note: Strollers are allowed in the museum and are also offered FREE of charge at the main entrance.

The Cincinnati Art Museum, founded in 1881, is one of the nation's oldest visual art institutions and the first general art museum west of the Allegheny Mountains to be established in its own building. In 1886 it opened its doors and was acclaimed to be "The Art Palace of the West."

The museum's featured collections offer the only collection of ancient Nabataean art outside of Jordan. In addition, it possesses the renowned Herbert Greer French collection of old master prints, a fine collection of European and American portrait miniatures, many paintings from Cincinnati's "Golden Age" (1830-1900), as well as Cincinnati's own Rookwood pottery and more than 40 pieces of Cincinnati carved furniture.

CIVIC GARDEN CENTER OF
GREATER CINCINNATI
Admission is FREE

- Open Mondays through Fridays from 9:00 a.m. - 4:00 p.m. and Saturdays from 9:00 a.m. - 3:00 p.m.
- Location: 2715 Reading Road · Cincinnati, OH 45206
- Phone: 513-221-0981
- Web Site: http://civicgardencenter.org

The Civic Garden Center delivers education in horticulture to children, adults and communities throughout the Cincinnati region. It has a library with more than 2,000 books about gardening and floral topics as well as videos and other resources. The Center has been instrumental in beautifying Greater Cincinnati with its urban gardening projects which have turned some 50 neglected properties into community gardens. Contact the Center to learn more about these neighborhood gardens and other botanical creations the Center has established around the area.

CLEVELAND BOTANICAL GARDEN
Admission is FREE

- Open April through October Mondays through Saturdays from 9:00 a.m. - Dusk and Sundays from Noon - Dusk. The Children's Garden closes at 5:00 p.m.
- Location: 11030 East Blvd. · Cleveland, OH 44106
- Phone: 216-721-1600
- Web Site: www.cbgarden.org

More than 10 beautiful acres of different natural and formal gardens make up the Cleveland Botanical Garden. And The Eleanor Armstrong Smith Glasshouse will open in late 2003. This glass conservatory will feature two very fragile ecosystems: The spiny desert of Madagascar and the cloud forest of Costa Rica making the CBG a year-round exhibit.

The permanent gardens include the Hershey Children's Garden, Japanese Garden, a rose garden, reading garden, herb garden and Woodland garden. The Hershey Children's Garden comes with a shooting-fountain that kids have been known to confuse with a sprinkler for their amusement, a large tree house with reading books, a fish pond and garden area where they can pot a small plant, fill buckets from the old-fashioned water pump and play with a number of other items.

Another treat for visitors is the Living Exhibit Gardens where there's a natural woodland waterfall, Aerie Overlook Garden, Cascade Garden, Enabling Garden, English Avenue Garden, Meditation Garden and Welcome Arbor Garden.

CLEVELAND CENTER FOR CONTEMPORARY ART

Admission is FREE on Fridays ONLY. Admission for children under 12-years-old is always FREE

- Open Tuesdays through Sundays from 11:00 a.m. - 6:00 p.m. (Thursdays' hours are extended to 8:00 p.m.). However, please note that the museum occasionally closes earlier than the posted times for special events. Parking costs may apply.
- Location: 8501 Carnegie Avenue · Cleveland, OH 44105
- Phone: 216-421-8671
- Web Site: www.contemporaryart.org

The Cleveland Center for Contemporary Art displays four seasons of exhibitions per year. It emphasizes progressive ideas that embrace a full spectrum of artistic issues, including vital political and social issues. Its wide-array of programs reflect cultural and artistic diversity celebrating national and international artistic achievements, as well as contributions by regional artists.

Founded in 1968 as The New Gallery by Marjorie Talalay, Agnes Gund and Nina Castelli Sundell, the New Gallery became the Cleveland Center for Contemporary Art in 1984. In 1990, the Center found its current 23,000 square-foot home in the former Sears building, which is part of the Cleveland Playhouse complex.

The Center has published approximately 50 scholarly exhibition catalogues receiving national recognition. And can be found at major art libraries and university and retail bookstores nationwide and abroad.

CLEVELAND MUSEUM OF ART
Admission is FREE

- Open Tuesdays, Thursdays, Saturdays and Sundays from 10:00 a.m. - 5:00 p.m. and Wednesdays and Fridays from 10:00 a.m. - 9:00 p.m. Closed Mondays, January 1, July 4, Thanksgiving Day, December 25
- Location: 11150 East Blvd., University Circle, Cleveland, OH 44106
- Phone: 216-421-7350
- Web Site: http://www.clemusart.com

The Cleveland Museum of Art is a leader in the international art world and offers many rich and diverse community, cultural and educational programming for the northeast Ohio area. Established in 1913 "for the benefit of all the people forever," the museum is one of the world's most distinguished and comprehensive art museums with the objective of reaching the broadest possible audience.

It also has rotating collections (collections that are not on permanent display because pieces may be sensitive to light or may be too fragile). Additional collections are also rotated in and out of the galleries throughout the year.

The Cleveland Museum of Art also offers many programs such as "If These Walls Could Talk," which features multicultural stories told by storytellers for FREE. Stories are told at 2:30 p.m. on the third Sunday of each month.

COLUMBUS MUSEUM OF ART
Admission is FREE ONLY on Thursday evenings

- Open Thursdays from 10:30 a.m. - 8:30 p.m. and Tuesdays through Sundays from 10:30 a.m. - 5:30 p.m. It is closed on Mondays. Please note that there is a $2 parking charge
- Location: 480 E. Broad Street · Columbus, OH 43215

- Phone: 614-221-6801 or 614-221-4848
- Web Site: www.cmaohio.org

The Columbus Museum of Art features works from its excellent collection of impressionists, German expressionists, cubists, American modernists, and contemporary art. The museum also includes works by Degas, Monet, Matisse, Picasso, Cassatt, Bellows, Demuth, Hopper, Marin, and O'Keeffe. Visitors may also take a stroll through the Russell Page Sculpture Garden or explore the world of photography in the Ross Photography Center. Families with children may also want to visit the interactive exhibit Eye Spy: Adventures in Art. In addition, there is a continuous program of national and international traveling exhibitions displayed at the museum.

COWAN POTTERY MUSEUM
Admission is FREE

- Open Mondays through Thursdays from 9:00 a.m. - 9:00 p.m; Fridays and Saturdays from 9:00 a.m. - 6:00 p.m. and Sundays from 1:00 p.m. - 5:00 p.m.
- Location: Rocky River Public Library · 1600 Hampton Road · Rocky River, OH 44116
- Phone: 440-333-7610
- Web Site: http://cowan.rrpl.org/main.php

The Cowan Pottery Museum has more than 1,100 pieces of R. Guy Cowan's works, the largest Cowan collection in the world. It is significant to American history because it bridged a transition from the arts and crafts movement in pottery - represented by Rookwood, Roseville and others - to the modern commodities epitomized by art deco designs of the Homer Laughlin Company, Fiesta Wares and others. The Cowan pottery was produced between 1912 and 1917. The museum also purchased the John Brodbeck private collection of more than 800 pieces.

DAWES ARBORETUM
Admission is FREE

- Open daily from Dawn - Dusk
- Location: 7770 Jacksontown Rd. SE · Newark, OH 43056
- Phone: 800-44-DAWES
- Web Site: www.dawesarb.org

This park covers approximately 1,150 acres of natural beauty. What was begun in 1929 by Beman and Bertie Dawes to demonstrate the value of trees and shrubbery has grown in epic proportions to become a showcase of plant collections and plethora of educational experiences. Some of the collections feature crab apples, conifers, oaks, azaleas and hollies. The grounds are accessible by an almost five-mile auto route and more than eight miles of hiking trails. Some feature attractions and visitor favorites include the remarkable cypress swamps, renowned Japanese Bonsai Garden and the "world's largest lettered hedges."

DAYTON ART INSTITUTE
Admission is FREE and so is parking

- Open 365 days per year from 10:00 a.m. - 5:00 p.m. (Thursdays until 9:00 p.m.)
- Location: 456 Belmonte Park North · Dayton, OH 45405
- Phone: 800-296-4426 or 937-223-5277
- Web Site: www.daytonartinstitute.org

The American Association of Museums rate The Dayton Art Institute, "superb in quality." There are more than 10,000 works in the permanent collection representing a wide variety of art history and cultures throughout the world. The collection features American, African, Asian and European art.

FRANKLIN PARK CONSERVATORY
AND BOTANICAL GARDEN
Only the Bonsai Courtyard and Palm House are FREE
(Admission fee required for anything else)

- Open Tuesdays through Sundays from 10:00 a.m. -
  5:00 p.m. (Wednesdays from 10:00 a.m. - 8:00 p.m.)
- Location: 1777 East Broad Street · Columbus,
  OH 43203
- Phone: 800-214-PARK
- Web Site: www.fpconservatory.org

This park includes 28 acres of themed gardens and landscaped
grounds but please note that only the Bonsai Courtyard and
Palm House are FREE. The Bonsai Courtyard displays many
bonsai trees, including the full-size ginkgo, pine and flowering
cherry trees. The garden is home to a pond filled with bloom-
ing water lilies and other plant life. The Palm House is a 100-
year-old architectural landmark containing tall palm trees,
ferns, fig trees and ancient cycads.

KENNEDY MUSEUM OF ART
Admission and parking are FREE

- Open Tuesdays, Wednesdays, Fridays, Saturdays and
  Sundays from Noon - 5:00 p.m and on Thursdays from
  Noon - 8:00 p.m. Closed on Mondays.
- Location: Ohio University · Lin Hall · Athens,
  OH 45701
- Phone: 740-593-1304
- Web Site: www.ohiou.edu/museum/

The Kennedy Museum of Art at Ohio University focuses its
collection on works of art that it has the resources and
capabilities to house, preserve and study. The museum is an
integral part of the educational, research and public service
missions of the university. Its purpose is to enhance the intel-

lectual and cultural life of the region by exhibiting quality, national and international exhibitions, collection-based research and diverse formal and informal learning opportunities.

KINGWOOD CENTER
Admission is FREE

- Open April through October from 8:00 a.m. - Dusk and until 5:00 p.m. the rest of the year
- Location: 900 Park Avenue West · Mansfield, OH 44906
- Phone: 419-522-0211

Visitors will enjoy the casual atmosphere of this 47-acre estate and its vibrantly colored gardens, greenhouse and mansion. The landscaped gardens have one of the largest tulip displays in the U.S. and the greenhouse provides year-round displays. Trails curl through woodlands and around ponds. And the French Provincial mansion still houses many original furnishings and one of the best libraries in the state for horticultural resources with more than 8,000 volumes.

KROHN CONSERVATORY
Admission is FREE

- Open daily from 10:00 a.m. - 5:00 p.m.
- Location: 1501 Eden Park Drive · Cincinnati, OH 45202
- Phone: 513-352-4080

One of Cincinnati's treasures, the Krohn Conservatory features Bonsai, Conservatory, Orchid, Tropical and Perennial gardens and collections. The total collection represents more than 1,000 different species of plants from rainforests to deserts. The best time to visit the Conservatory is in autumn. This is when butterflies are invited to invade the Conservatory and fly freely around, adding more radiant colors for visitors to enjoy.

LICKING COUNTY ART GALLERY
FREE admission

- Open Tuesdays through Sundays from 1:00 p.m. - 4:00 p.m.
- Closed Mondays and holidays
- Location: 391 Hudson Avenue · Newark, OH
- Phone: 740-349-8031

The Licking County Art Gallery schedules shows featuring local artists.

MOUNT AIRY FOREST AND ARBORETUM
Admission is FREE

- Open daily from Dawn - Dusk
- Location: 5083 Colerain Avenue · Mount Airy, OH in Greater Cincinnati
- Phone: 513-352-4094

Mount Airy is said to be the first municipal reforestation project in the country and is still the nations largest municipal park. More than one million trees were planted across approximately 1,500 acres in the early Twentieth Century. The Arboretum is a one-story brick building reflecting the architectural style of Frank Lloyd Wright - although he was not the architect. It displays flowering crab apple trees, azaleas, lilacs and rhododendrons. The grounds cover a wide-array of landscape ranging from rolling hills, valleys, streams, gardens, woods and wildlife. The park also has many other out buildings. One point of interest is the Garden Totem greeting visitors. It is an abstract sculpture of inspired plant forms made of stainless steel.

PARK OF ROSES
Admission is FREE

- Open daily from Dawn - Dusk.
- Location: Whetstone Park · 3923 High Street · Columbus, OH 43214.
- Phone: 614-645-3222

This 13-acre treasure of Columbus contains more than 11,000 rose bushes covering more than 350 varieties of roses. It is one of the largest municipal rose gardens in the U.S. In addition, the park has herb, perennial and daffodil gardens as well. The daffodil garden features 1,000 varieties. The best times of the year to visit are the middle of June or the middle of September to really take in the breath-taking beauty as the roses are in full bloom. Several events take place annually, including musical programs in the evenings throughout the summer and an annual rose festival in June.

RIFFE GALLERY
Admission is FREE

- Open Mondays and Tuesdays from 10:00 a.m. - 4:00 p.m.; Wednesdays and Fridays from 10:00 a.m. - 8:00 p.m.; Saturdays from Noon - 8:00 p.m. and Sundays from Noon - 4:00 p.m.
- Location: 77 S. High St. · Columbus, OH 43215 (In the Verne Riffe Center for the Government of Arts across the street from the Ohio Statehouse)
- Phone: 614-644-9624
- Web Site: http://www.oac.state.oh.us/riffegallery/

This museum showcases Ohio artists' collections of works. It also has collections displayed that are from various other Ohio art institutions. A rotating series of four shows display other works arranged by different museum curators throughout the year. The Riffe Gallery is owned and operated by the Ohio Art Council.

ROCKEFELLER PARK,
GARDENS AND GREENHOUSE
Admission is FREE

- Open daily from 10:00 a.m. - 4:00 p.m.
- Location: 750 E. 88th Street · Cleveland, OH 44108
- Phone: 216-664-3103

Come see the garden than talks. These four acres of gardens and show houses have recorded descriptions of the plants around. Visitors are urged to touch and smell the foliage. Outdoor gardens include Japanese and Peach gardens and seasonal displays. Indoors, you'll find a water garden, tropical plants, fruits and seasonal flowers. In addition, there's a cactus House, Fern Room and much more.

Nearby are the Cleveland Cultural Gardens in Rockefeller Park along Martin Luther King Jr. Drive. Visitors may drive or walk through some 25 gardens representing different nationalities. These landscape treasures are each distinctive in their own way and commemorate the city's ethnic diversity.

ROMANIAN ETHNIC ART MUSEUM
Admission is FREE

- Open by appointment only
- Location: 3256 Warren Road · Cleveland, OH 44111
- Phone: 216-941-5550

The museum is housed in the Hall of St. Mary's Church and is only open for guided tours by appointment. Inside, visitors will see wonderful displays of folk costumes, beads and sequins, carved wood and ceramics, sculptures and paintings, religious icons and ecclesiastical vestments and accessories. In addition there is a historical photo-book and other pieces.

ROSS C. PURDY MUSEUM OF CERAMICS
Admission is FREE

- Open Mondays through Fridays from 9:00 a.m. - 5:00 p.m.
- Location: 735 Ceramic Place · Westerville, OH 43086
- Phone: 614-890-4700
- Web Site: http://www.acers.org/acers/museum.asp

One hundred and fifty years of ceramic history is preserved at this museum. It features 2,000 pieces representing anything from traditional to high-tech ceramic art. And in the lobby, sits the world's largest crystal ball. The museum also displays many high-tech items such as tile from the Space Shuttle, military armor, ceramic body parts and more. The museum's library contains more than 10,000 books covering just about anything ceramic related.

SOUTHERN OHIO HOME AND GARDEN SHOW
Admission is FREE

- When: March
- Location: Ross County Fairgrounds in Chillicothe, OH
- Phone: 800-413-4118

If you are looking for home decorating ideas or landscaping insight, come to the Southern Ohio Home and Garden Show. Local home and garden merchants display exhibits and arrangements for visitors to browse and strike up conversation over tips and tricks for their green-thumb.

SPRINGFIELD ART MUSEUM
Admission is FREE

- Open Tuesdays, Thursdays and Fridays from 9:00 a.m. - 5:00 p.m.; Wednesdays from 9:00 a.m. - 9:00 p.m;

Saturdays from 9:00 a.m. - 3:00 p.m. and Sundays
from 2:00 p.m. - 4:00 p.m. Closed on Mondays.

- Location: 107 Cliff Park Road · Springfield, OH 45501
- Phone: 937-325-4673
- Web Site: www.spfld-museum-of-art.org

The Springfield Museum of Art has seven galleries. Its permanent collection includes paintings, drawings and sculptures
featuring 19th and 20th century American, European and Ohio
artists. The museum also has about 12 changing exhibits annually. These exhibits address contemporary and historical issues
and encourage critical understanding of the visual arts.

STEUBENVILLE MURALS
Admission is FREE

- Open anytime
- Location: Steubenville, OH
- Phone: 800-510-4442 or 740-283-4935

If you like outdoor art or graffiti, then make a trip to the little
Ohio downtown of Steubenville to see the murals painted in
various locations throughout the city. This is like a city's history being told in pictures painted on the sides of buildings.
Some 30 or more giant murals can be seen. Call for details
regarding where these outdoor art exhibits can be found.

STRANAHAN ARBORETUM
Admission is FREE

- Open April through October Mondays through Fridays
  from 9:00 a.m. - 2:00 p.m. And on Saturdays from
  June through September from 10:00 a.m. - 4:00 p.m.
  Also, in May and October, its open Saturdays and
  Sundays from 1:00 p.m. - 5:00 p.m.
- Location: 4131 Tantara Drive · Toledo, OH 43623

- Phone: 419-841-1007
- Web Site: http://arboretum.utoledo.edu

This 47-acre site features an excellent collection of rare trees, a ravine, wetlands and a restored prairie. The best times of year to visit are May to see the wildflowers in full bloom and October to see the autumn colors. The more than 1,500 trees include a variety of North American pine, oak, maple and buckeye. However, more interesting trees from China, Japan, Norway and Serbia are also prevalent. The arboretum is run by the University of Toledo and is located within the Oak Openings sand dune region. Appropriately, peaks of old sand dunes are still visible above the forest's undergrowth.

TAFT MUSEUM OF ART
Admission is FREE on Wednesdays ONLY

- Open from Mondays through Saturdays from 10:00 a.m. - 5:00 p.m. and Sundays from 1:00 p.m. - 5:00 p.m.
- Location: 316 Pike St. · Cincinnati, OH 45202
- Phone: 513-241-0343
- Web Site: www.taftmuseum.org

This museum is housed in the former home of Charles and Anna Taft. Charles was the half-brother of President Howard Taft. On display is a wide variety of sculpture, ceramics, jewelry and art pieces from around the globe and throughout history. In addition, special traveling exhibits are also displayed periodically throughout the year. The renovated museum opens in spring of 2003.

TEMPLE MUSEUM OF RELIGIOUS ART
Admission is FREE

- Museum tours are available by appointment Mondays through Fridays from 9:00 a.m. - 4:00 p.m.

- Location: Temple-Tifereth Israel, a national landmark building in University Circle at Silver Park in Cleveland, OH
- Phone: 216-831-3233
- Web Site: www.ttti.org/

The Temple Museum is the fourth oldest museum of Judaica in the country. Founded in 1950, it now has one of the most prominent and comprehensive collections of religious and Judaic art. Its collections include antique Torah hangings used in European synagogues that date to the seventeenth century; silver Torah ornaments, antiquities and household pottery from the Holy Land region dating from 2000 B.C.E. to Roman times; fold art objects made and used by Jews in many countries; many historic documents, manuscripts and bibles; and a collection of sculptures, paintings and lithographs by famous Jewish artists.

THE CONTEMPORARY ARTS CENTER
Admission is FREE on Mondays ONLY

- Open Mondays through Saturdays from 10:00 a.m. - 6:00 p.m. and Sundays from Noon - 5:00 p.m.
- Location: 115 E. Fifth St. · Cincinnati, OH 45202
- Phone: 513-345-8400
- Web Site: www.spiral.org

This art museum focuses on the latest progress made in new media, performance art, photography, architecture, painting and sculpture. The gallery also exhibits multimedia and video mediums of art.

TOLEDO BOTANICAL GARDEN
Admission is FREE

- Open April through September from 8:00 a.m. -

9:00 p.m. and October through March from 8:00 a.m. - 6:00 p.m.

- Location: 5403 Elmer Drive · Toledo, OH 43615.
- Phone: 419-936-2987.
- Web Site: www.toledogarden.org

Gardens and meadows cover some 57-acres of land where a variety of plant life thrive, including wildflowers and roses. This botanical garden is actually a series of different gardens within a garden. The feature sights include a greenhouse, village garden, shade garden, and herb garden with a wonderful fragrance wafting in the breeze. It also features a pioneer garden, vegetable and flower gardens, and perennials. Other points of interest are the outdoor sculpture collection and artists studios and galleries. Lastly, there is a café and gift shop for visitors to relax and enjoy.

TOLEDO MUSEUM OF ART
Admission is FREE. Parking costs $2

- Open Tuesdays through Thursdays from 10:00 a.m. - 4:00 p.m; Fridays 10:00 a.m. - 10:00 p.m; Saturdays from 10:00 a.m. - 4:00 p.m. and Sundays from 11:00 a.m. - 5:00 p.m. Closed Mondays, New Year's Day, Independence Day, Thanksgiving Day and Christmas Day
- Location: 2445 Monroe Street · Toledo, OH 43620
- Phone: 800-644-6862 or 419-255-8000
- Web Site: www.toledomuseum.org

The Toledo Museum of Art has one of the finest collections in the country with more than 30,000 works from places across the globe and nearly every period. Pieces of its collection are often featured in publications and displayed in traveling exhibitions.

The collection includes African art, American painting, Ancient art, Asian art, decorative arts and sculptures, European paintings, glass, graphic arts, and modern and contemporary art.

TOPIARY GARDEN
Admission is FREE

- Open daily from sunrise - sunset
- Location: Old Deaf School Park · Columbus, OH (Corner of East Town Street and Washington Avenue)
- Phone: 614-645-0197
- Web Site: www.topiarygarden.org

This unique arts project was conceived by James T. Mason's recreation of Georges Seurat's famous post-impressionist painting - A Sunday On The Island Of La Grande Jatte - in topiary (sculpted shrubbery) with giant human figures. There are a total of 54 topiary people, eight boats, several dogs, a cat and monkey. The largest figure stands about 12-feet. Visitors are encouraged to bring a camera and enjoy an afternoon picnic amongst the outdoor topiary sculptures and natural pond.

WEGERZYN GARDENS
& HORTICULTURE CENTER
Admission is FREE

- Open Mondays through Fridays fro9m 9:00 a.m. - 5:00 p.m.
- Location: 1301 E. Siebenthaler Avenue · Dayton, OH
- Phone: 937-277-6545
- Web Site: http://www.metroparks.org/Facilities/ Wegerzyn_Gardens_MetroPark/wegerzyn _gardens_metropark.html

The Miami Valley's Five Rivers Metroparks in Southwest Ohio is home to the Wegerzyn Gardens and Horticulture

Center. It features Victorian, English, Federal and Children's Rose gardens and has a boardwalk that allows visitors to see rivers and forest. In addition, there is a Reception Lawn amidst a wall of pine trees, a nature trail allowing people to see wild natural habitats for plant life and wildlife. Also, a scenic river bikeway and a learning center are nearby. The learning center offers opportunities to obtain instructional insight regarding home landscaping, gardening and floral craft making. One of the main attractions is the Children's Discovery Garden, which includes a preschool area, two ponds, individual garden plots, wildlife area, perennial and rock gardens.

WEXNER CENTER FOR THE ARTS
FREE on Thursdays ONLY after 5:00 p.m.

- Open Thursdays from 10:00 a.m. - 9:00 p.m; Sundays from Noon - 6:00 p.m and Tuesdays, Wednesdays, Fridays and Saturdays from 10:00 a.m. - 6:00 p.m. Closed on Mondays
- Location: The Ohio State University · 1871 North High Street · Columbus, OH 43210
- Phone: 614-292-3535
- Web Site: www.wexarts.org

The Wexner Center opened in 1989 and is now one of the few multidisciplinary contemporary arts centers in the country. Although it was originally conceived as a research laboratory for all of the arts, it emphasizes commissions for new works and artist residencies. Its multidisciplinary programs encompass performing arts, exhibitions, media arts and worldwide cutting-edge culture.

The Wexner exhibitions feature art and ideas of an international array of contemporary artists working in a range of media including painting, sculpture, architecture, photography and multimedia installations.

ZANESVILLE ART CENTER
Admission is FREE

- Open Tuesdays, Wednesdays and Fridays from 10:00 a.m. - 5:00 p.m; Thursdays from 10:00 a.m. - 8:30 p.m.; Saturdays and Sundays from 1:00 p.m. - 5:00 p.m.
- Location: 620 Military Road · Zanesville, OH 43701
- Phone: 740-452-0741
- Web Site: www.zanesvilleartcenter.org

The Zanesville Art Center will make you feel like your going back in time when you enter its 300-year-old English panel room, which was dismantled and brought to America by William Randolph Hearst. The Center features masterpieces by Turner, Rembrandt and Rubens. Traveling exhibits include Asian art, rare pieces of American glass and one of the oldest collections of children's art around.

OOH-AHH-EE-AH-HA
(Halls of Fame & Museums)

Well, what do you say when you see things that you've never seen before?

We have all heard of the Rock and Roll or Pro Football Halls of Fame but did you know Ohio's also home to the Barbers and Trap Shooting Halls of Fame? And they're free to visit.

Ohio's museums are pretty unique too. There are places dedicated to paperweights, telephones and the history of the vacuum cleaner to name a few.

So stop hemmin' & hawin' and get to these intrastate gems. And you too will say silly things like "ooh" and "ahh." If not, then you're sure to say something like "ee" or "ah-ha!"

AKRON POLICE MUSEUM
Admission is FREE

- Open Mondays through Fridays from 8:00 a.m. - 3:30 p.m.
- Location: Harold K. Stubbs Justice Center · Mezzanine Level · 217 South High St. · Akron, OH 44308
- Phone: 330-375-2390
- Web Site: www.ci.akron.oh.us/police06.html

This museum features confiscated weapons of all kinds, and gambling and narcotics paraphernalia. It also displays counterfeit money and police related accessories, including uniforms and weapons. Hundreds of historic photographs are also available for public viewing. The museum also has a vintage 1965 Harley-Davidson police motorcycle and keys to its original 1890 jail cell.

AMERICAN CLASSICAL MUSIC HALL OF FAME AND MUSEUM
Admission is FREE

- Open Mondays through Fridays from 9:00 a.m. - 4:30 p.m.
- Location: 4 West Fourth St. · Cincinnati, OH 45202
- Phone: 513-621-3263 or 800-499-3263
- Web Site: www.classicalhall.org

Celebrate the history of classical music at this national institution honoring the best of American classical music's performance artists. It recognizes individuals who have impacted symphonies, orchestras, schools and conservatories, both past and present. It also provides visitors with recordings to listen to the works of the Hall's inductees. In addition, there are many displays of classical music memorabilia, famous instruments, a bugle collection and stained glass from various opera houses.

AMERICAN WATCHMAKERS INSTITUTE
HISTORY OF TIME MUSEUM
Admission is FREE

- Open Mondays through Fridays from 9:00 a.m. - 5:00 p.m.
- Location: 701 Enterprise Drive · Harrison, OH 45030
- Phone: 513-367-2924

If you just like to watch time go by, this museum is just the place to do it. It celebrates, what else, the science of time known as horology. It has interesting exhibits displayed such as rope clocks and sundials to modern-day watches. In addition, there are plenty of pocket-watches, ship chronometers and anything else with a face and hands to measure time.

AUMAN MUSEUM OF RADIO AND TV
Admission is FREE

- Open by appointment only
- Location: 4316 Murray Road · Dover, OH 44622
- Phone: 330-364-1058
- Web Site: http://www.geocities.com/TelevisionCity/ Set/1930/

This personal collection of vintage radio and television history is the result of curator Larry Auman's 40-year quest. It includes more than 300 different television sets covering every era. It includes the 1930s "Mechanical Era and the 1950s "Golden Age of TV." In addition, hundreds of comic books, games, toys and more are on display.

BARBERS HALL-OF-FAME MUSEUM
Admission is FREE

- Open by appointment only
- Location: Above Zeke's Barber Shop at 2½ South

High St. in Canal Winchester, OH

- Phone: 614-837-1556 or 614-837-5311

For not advertising or promoting this Ohio gem, owner/curator and retired barber Edwin Jeffers has had visitors from more than 40 states and five countries. The museum is one-of-a-kind. It features 58 barber poles, barber chairs from six eras, re-created barber shops from eras past, hundreds of mugs and razors that are hundreds of years old, and blood-letting and tooth-pulling tools that were used long ago when barbers sometimes moonlighted as surgeons and dentists. It's no wonder Mr. Jeffers has appeared on many cable television shows, including a Japanese station.

BOONSHOFT MUSEUM OF DISCOVERY
(Dayton Museum of Natural History)
*Admission is FREE on the third Tuesday of each
month from 4:00 p.m. - 9:00 p.m. ONLY*

- Location: 2600 DeWeese Pkwy. · Dayton, OH 45414
- Phone: 937-275-7431
- Web Site: www.boonshoftmuseum.org

You probably won't see it advertised but this wonderful museum is free to visit, if only for four hours per month. And it has a lot to offer kids and adults alike. This science museum has nearly 1.5 million items in its collection of artifacts and live specimens. The adventure in the world of science includes a visit to Science Central where air, water and motion education occurs. An eagle view is awaiting at the top of the Tree Top Pavilion and Ohio wildlife await visitors in the Wild Ohio indoor zoo. Take the Eco Trek and learn about a variety of environments found on Earth and explore out of this world discoveries in the Space Theater. If you have children six-years-old or younger, you can introduce them to snakes, a bobcat and coyote in the Kid's Corner and nature area.

BUTCH'S COCA-COLA MUSEUM
Admission is FREE

- Open Tuesdays through Sundays from 10:00 a.m. - 5:00 p.m.
- Location: Harmon Village at 118 Maple St.
  · Marietta, OH 45750
- Phone: 740-376-2653
- Web Site: http://www.harmarvillage.com/harmarcoke/ cokemuseum/cokemuseum.html

Seeing the history of Coca-Cola and all kinds of Coke memorabilia through the ages is like traveling through American history and "pop" culture. The collection of Coca-Cola artifacts amassed by Butch Badgett is a site to see. Butch's father handcrafted many of the unique Cola items found in the Cola shop from wood. The museum features many collectibles such as dolls, carry-on airline coolers, billfolds, an aluminum bottle carrier, signs, tins, dinner ware, machines, clothing and just about anything else you could imagine from the 1920s to present.

CLEVELAND POLICE HISTORICAL MUSEUM
Admission is FREE

- Open Mondays through Fridays from 10:00 a.m. - 4:00 p.m.
- Location: Cleveland Justice Center · 1300 Ontario St.
  · Cleveland, OH 44113
- Phone: 216-523-5055
- Web Site: www.clevelandpolicemuseum.org

This police museum has a wide variety of arresting displays and artifacts, including death masks, motorcycles, the first call box and case files and police blotters dating back to 1866. Many photographs and scrapbooks depict chilling notorious crime stories in the area's history. In addition, the museum highlights Eliot Ness, weapons, mounted units and a Hall-of-Fame. Another point of interest is the first closed-circuit camera used in banks, which is displayed at the museum.

CROATIAN HERITAGE MUSEUM
Admission is FREE

- Open Fridays from 7:00 p.m. - 10:00 p.m. and Sundays from 2:00 p.m. - 5:00 p.m.
- Location: 34900 Lakeshore Blvd. · Eastlake, OH 44095
- Phone: 440-946-2044

This museum represents Croatian-American cultural history and has exhibits promoting appreciation for Croatia descendents. Many traveling collections are also featured at this museum throughout the year.

DEGENHART PAPERWEIGHT AND GLASS MUSEUM
Admission is FREE only for those under 18-years-old. Otherwise, it's $1.50

- Open Mondays through Saturdays from 9:00 a.m. - 5:00 p.m. and Sundays from 1:00 p.m. - 5:00 p.m.
- Location: Highland Hill Road · Cambridge, OH 43725
- Phone: 740-432-2626

See the personal collection of Elizabeth Degenhart, owner of the world famous Crystal Art Glass Company. It features Degenhart glass, cruets and paperweights in brightly lit exhibits creating beautiful sparkle. There are also many pieces of Midwestern pattern glass on display and a video presentation about glass making.

DITTRICK MUSEUM OF MEDICAL HISTORY
Admission is FREE

- Open Mondays through Fridays from 10:00 a.m. - 4:30 p.m. only
- Location: Third Floor of the Allen Memorial Medical Library · 11000 Euclid Avenue (Corner of Euclid Avenue and Adelbert Road) · Cleveland, OH 44106
- Phone: 216-368-6391
- Web Site: www.cwru.edu/artsci/dittrick/museum.htm

This museum of medical history will make visitors marvel at the medical advancements made or have a coronary to think how archaic today's medical devices may look to future generations. The collection has more than 10,000 images and 60,000 rare books and museum objects. Artifacts displayed represent medical history from 1800 through 1965, including items such as a 1952 infant respirator, 1928 X-ray machine, 1861 amputating set, 1882 antiseptic sprayer, 1890 surgical chair and much more. The museum's displays also include an 1870's and 1930's doctors' offices, 1880's pharmacy and hospital medicines from 1865 - 1920.

GLASS HERITAGE MUSEUM
Admission is FREE

- Open Tuesdays through Saturdays from 10:00 a.m. - 4:00 p.m. only
- Location: 109 North Main Street · Fostoria, OH 44830
- Phone: 419-435-5077

Fostoria, Ohio had 13 glass factories from 1887 - 1920. The museum today has more than 1,000 glass artifacts from that period by those companies. The colorful displays feature clear, three-layered and prism colored glass and more. Fostoria provided 60 percent of all manufactured kerosene lamps in America once upon a time. These included large, small and multi-colored models. Another attraction is the tableware displayed at the museum.

HOOVER HISTORICAL CENTER
Admission is FREE

- Open Tuesdays through Sundays from 1:00 p.m. - 5:00 p.m.
- Location: 1875 Easton St. N.W., North Canton, OH 44720
- Phone: 330-499-0287
- Web Site: www.hoover.com

This museum will "suck" you in. In fact, it has "sweeping" displays demonstrating the history of the vacuum cleaner. And it's the only known museum of its kind. The collection is found in the boyhood home of William H. "Boss" Hoover, founder of Hoover Vacuums. The interesting exhibits will make you feel for your grandparents as you imagine them using these relics of "good housekeeping." Tours are held on the hour from 1 - 4 p.m. And the Hoover Center also has a garden open to tours and special events throughout the year, including storytelling, a Halloween storytelling festival and Christmas activities.

JAMES M. THOMAS TELEPHONE MUSEUM
Admission is FREE

- Open Mondays through Fridays from 8:30 a.m. - 4:30 p.m.
- Location: 68 East Main Street · Chillicothe, OH 45601
- Phone: 740-772-8200

James M. Thomas pioneered the non-Bell independent telephone industry and this museum is dedicated to his accomplishments. It features a wooden underground conduit, which contained early Western Union cables that ran beneath the streets of Chillicothe. And an old switchboard, phone directories as early as 1897 and many other telephone equipment are displayed.

KNOX COUNTY AGRICULTURAL MUSEUM
Admission is FREE

- Open by appointment only
- Location: Knox County Fairgrounds · Mount Vernon, OH 43050
- Phone: 740-397-1423

This agricultural museum captures Ohio farm-life during the 1800's and early 1900's. It has more than 3,000 pieces exhibited, including household items, farming tools and machinery, a one-room schoolhouse and a log house.

MANSFIELD FIRE MUSEUM
Admission is FREE

- Open June 1st through September 1st Saturdays through Wednesdays from 1:00 p.m. - 4:00 p.m. and from September to June on Saturdays and Sundays only from 1:00 p.m. - 4:00 p.m.
- Location: 1265 West Fourth Street · Mansfield, OH 44906
- Phone: 419-529-2573 or 800-211-7231
- Web Site: www.mansfieldfiremuseum.org

The museum itself is a reproduction of a turn-of-the-century firehouse where firefighters hitched their fire-wagons to horses. The museum opens the window to a fascinating history of firefighting and the people, tools and lifestyle of these brave public servants. Visitors will feel as if they took a step back into time.

MOTORCYCLE HALL OF FAME MUSEUM
Admission is FREE for those 17-years-old or younger ONLY

- Open daily from 9:00 a.m. - 5:00 p.m.
- Location: 13515 Yarmouth Dr. · Pickerington, OH 43147
- Phone: 614-856-2222
- Web Site: www.ama-cycle.org/museum

It seems Americans have always been intrigued by the mystique of riding the open roads, freely, on a motorcycle. Here, you will get to see some of the most famous bikers of all time and the road machines that they used. Inductees to the Hall include those who contributed significantly to the engineering, designing, business, history and of course riding of motorcycles. The Hall features more than 200 people who've been enshrined. In addition, there are three more exhibit halls that convey the history of the industry and folklore through displays of riding gear, pictures, sculptures, reconstructed racetracks, awards, literature posters and more. Motorcycling heritage is also evident in the fantastic traveling exhibits that appear throughout the year such as A Century of Indian - featuring Indian-model motorcycle history.

MUSEUM OF POSTAL HISTORY
Admission is FREE

- Open by appointment Mondays - Fridays
- Location: Lower level of the Delphos Post Office at 131 N. Main St. · Delphos, OH 45833
- Phone: 419-695-2811

Ready to go postal? Bad joke, I know. Anyway, visit the museum of postal history. Here, visitors can see a 1906 Harrington Rural Mail Coach and see additional displays covering some 7,000 square feet. It includes memorabilia and media presentations regarding the progress made in American mail history. Stamps, letters and postmarks are just some of what's here. Other highlights include a research library and films available in a mini-theater.

NATIONAL CLEVELAND-STYLE POLKA HALL-OF-FAME
Admission is FREE

- Open Mondays, Tuesdays, Thursdays and Fridays from Noon - 5:00 p.m. and Saturdays from 10:00 a.m. - 2:00 p.m. (Closed Wednesdays and Sundays)
- Location: Shore Cultural Centre · 291 East 222 St.
- Euclid, OH 44123
- Phone: 216-261-FAME or 866-66POLKA
- Web Site: www.clevelandstyle.com

Okay polka lovers, if you haven't made your pilgrimage to this hall-of-fame, plan on it. Memorabilia from America's Polka King - Frank Yankovic to turn-of-the-Century artifacts fill the collection at this museum. In addition to Yankovic's stage outfits and accordion, visitors will see Johnny Vadnal's accordion and other personal items, a video library and dedications to the greatest all-time hits, lifetime achievement honors, and pieces from Johnny Pecon and Eddie Habat.

N. K. WHITNEY STORE MUSEUM
Admission is FREE

- Open Mondays through Saturdays from 9:00 a.m. - Dusk and Sundays from 11:30 a.m. - Dusk
- Location: 8876 Chillicothe Road · Kirtland, OH 44094
- Phone: 440-256-9805

Okay, so you've been to Cracker Barrel but this is a truly authentic restored 1830s country store and post office. It features more than a thousand items and replicas of merchandise

that lured shoppers more than 150 years ago. Whitney's
General Store was the very first store in the Kirtland region.

OHIO CRAFT MUSEUM
Admission is FREE

- Open Mondays through Fridays from 10:00 a.m. -
  5:00 p.m. and Sundays from 1:00 p.m. - 5:00 p.m.
- Location: 1665 W. Fifth Ave. · Columbus, OH 43212
- Phone: 614-486-4402

The Ohio Craft Museum's exhibitions features Contemporary
American Crafts Artwork. It includes displays of works created in ceramics, glass, wood, fiber and metal.

OHIO SOCIETY OF MILITARY HISTORY
Admission is FREE

- Open Tuesdays through Fridays from 10:00 a.m. -
  5:00 p.m. and Saturdays from 10:00 a.m. - 3:00 p.m.
- Location: 316 Lincoln Way East · Massilon, OH 44646
- Phone: 330-832-5553

This museum honors the men and women who served and
fought in our nation's armed forces. It features many old uniforms, historic documents, prestigious medals and interesting
photographs. The memorabilia covers all periods of Ohio's
military history. In addition, it is home to the memorial honoring First Lieutenant Sharon A. Lane, who died on June 8,
1969 in Vietnam.

OHIO WOMEN'S HALL-OF-FAME
Admission is FREE

- Open during normal hours of the state government
- Location: 145 South Front St. · Columbus, OH 43215

- Phone: 614-466-4496
- Web Site: http://www.state.oh.us/odjfs/women/ Halloffame/index.stm

The Ohio Women's Hall-of-Fame was established in 1978 to honor and recognize the outstanding contributions by Ohio's women throughout the state's history. The Hall has approximately 330 inductees. It is a very inspirational exhibit for anyone but especially for women and young ladies. The legacy left by each of the Hall's members is remembered with the displays recognizing their achievements. Regional displays are open to visitors in Athens, Canton, Cincinnati, Cleveland, Mount Vernon, Toledo and Xenia. And a video - Women In Ohio History - is also available.

ORTON GEOLOGICAL MUSEUM
Admission is FREE

- Open Mondays through Fridays from 9:00 a.m. - 5:00 p.m.
- Location: Orton Hall on Ohio State University's main campus at 155 S. Oval · Columbus, OH 43210
- Phone: 614-292-6896

Some may think of this museum as Ohio's little Jurassic Park. After all, it features a full-size replica of a Tyrannosaurus Rex scull, a skeleton of a giant ground sloth and teeth from a Mastodon and Mammoth. But that's only the beginning, as visitors will find other eye-opening exhibits such as fluorescent minerals, crystals, fossils and a meteorite that fell in Ohio. Tell the kids your going to a museum of Ohio's "rock" history and open the fascinating world of geology to them. Tours are available upon request.

SPIRIT OF '76 MUSEUM
Admission is FREE

- Open from April 1 through October 31 on Saturdays and Sundays from 2:30 p.m. - 5:00 p.m. by appointment
- Location: 201 N. Main St. · Wellington, OH 44090
- Phone: 440-647-4576

Come see the celebrated history of painter Archibald Willard, artist of the famous "Spirit of '76." This painting is considered by many to be the nation's most inspirational painting of all-time. Willard spent most of his life painting in northeastern Ohio. In 1875, influenced by the death of his father, he decided to do the very serious piece depicting the American Revolutionary, which became famous. In addition to the many paintings by Willard, the museum contains Revolutionary and Civil War artifacts.

STENGEL-TRUE MUSEUM
Admission is FREE

- Open Saturdays and Sundays from 1:00 p.m. - 4:30 p.m.
- Location: Washington and State Streets in Marion, OH 43302
- Phone: 740-382-2826

This museum home was built in 1864. It features firearm collections from the Revolutionary War, Civil War and other wars. It also displays Indian artifacts, pottery and glassware, a collection of primitive light fixtures, antique clocks and children's toys. The interior of the home includes ornate architecture such as a fine Italian marble fireplace. In general, the museum has a very fine collection of antiques.

TIFFIN GLASS MUSEUM
Admission is FREE

- Open Tuesdays through Saturdays from 1:00 p.m. - 5:00 p.m.
- Location: 25 South Washington St. · Tiffin, OH 44883
- Phone: 419-448-0200
- Web Site: www.tiffinglass.org

The Tiffin Glass Club honors the heritage of Tiffin's Glass House by exhibiting 2,000 pieces of Tiffin glass at the museum to preserve the town and glass company heritage. The factory ran from 1889 to 1984. The museum features memorabilia, historic documents, popular Tiffin Glass lines, stemware, lamps, optics and more. The items are displayed in chronological order in beautiful wood cabinets.

TOLEDO FIREFIGHTERS MUSEUM
Admission is FREE

- Open on Saturdays from Noon - 4:00 p.m.
- Location: 918 Sylvania Avenue · Toledo, OH 43612
- Phone: 419-478-3473
- Web site: www.toledofiremuseum.com

This museum will provide its visitors with an opportunity to learn about fire safety and experience Toledo firefighting history. It features vintage pumpers and the uniforms and equipment used by the areas earliest firefighters.

TRAP SHOOTING HALL-OF-FAME
Admission is FREE

- Open October 1 - April 30 Mondays through Fridays from 9:00 a.m. - 4:00 p.m. And May 1 - September 30 Mondays through Fridays from 9:00 a.m. - 4:00 p.m.
- Location: 601 West National Road · Vandalia, OH 45377

- Phone: 937-898-4638
- Web Site: www.traphof.org

I never thought there was such a thing but believe me, this hall-of-fame museum is very real. In 1924, Vandalia, Ohio became the permanent host and home of the Grand American Trapshooting Tournament complete with official dedication ceremonies and inductions to the Hall. The museum's displays depict the history of trap shooting from the pigeon shoots in the 1800s to modern-day clay shoots. Displays include bizarre looking catapult machines, glass target balls, trap gun collections (including Olympic Medal Winners) and many more artifacts and memorabilia.

UKRANIAN MUSEUM AND ARCHIVES
Admission is FREE

- Call for hours
- Location: 1202 Kenilworth Avenue · Cleveland, OH 44113
- Phone: 216-781-4329
- Web Site: www.umacleveland.org

Ukranians and others have come from all around to attend events and see the museum and archives dedicated to preserving the history and culture of Ukraine. One of the most popular displays in the museum is the Easter eggs or Pysanky. The books and periodical section of the museum's archives cover a vast range of topics spanning Ukranian prehistory to modern headlines around the world.

WYANDOT POPCORN MUSEUM
Admission is FREE

- Open May 1 - October 31 from Wednesdays through Sundays from 1:00 p.m. - 4:00 p.m. And November 1 - April 30 from Saturdays through Sundays from

1:00 p.m. - 4:00 p.m.

- Location: Heritage Hall · 169 E. Church St. · Marion, OH 43302.
- Phone: 740-387-4255.
- Web Site: www.wyandotpopcornmus.com

Pop on over to see the largest collection of popcorn poppers and peanut roasters in the world. There's an 1890 Patent Olsen Squirrel Cage Dry Popper, 1899 Cretan popcorn machine, Ringling Brothers Circus's 1909 Cretors popcorn Wagon, 1927 concession truck and 1908 Dunbar Concession Wagon once used by Paul Newman to promote his own popcorn in Central Park. These and more than 50 other popcorn and peanut vending antiques are restored and look practically brand new.

YE OLD MILL
Admission is FREE

- Open daily May through October from 11:00 a.m. - 9:00 p.m.
- Location: 11324 SR-13, Utica, OH, 43080
- Phone: 740-892-3921
- Web Site: www.velvet-icecream.com

This beautiful historic old mill, complete with water-wheel, is home to the Velvet-Ice Cream Company. The mill was built in 1817. The museum inside provides visitors with a taste of how ice cream is made. There is no better time or place to grab a cone than Utica, Ohio in the heat of summer.

DON'T KNOW NOTHIN' 'BOUT HISTORY
(Historical Museums)

Just about every community in Ohio has a local history museum. If you haven't been to the nearest one to you - go. And if you have, visit one in another community.

Each local history museum has something unique in its collection. Case-in-point, Mastodon bones were found in a farmer's field and are now displayed at the local museum. By the way, it's free to see.

Chances are, with the mobility of our modern culture, few of us have taken advantage of the treasures found in our own backyards. And fewer still probably know much about (their local) history.

ALLEN COUNTY MUSEUM
Admission is FREE

- Open Tuesdays through Sundays from 1:00 p.m. - 5:00 p.m. (It opens at 10:00 a.m. from Tuesdays - Saturdays during June, July and August)
- Location: 620 West Market St. · Lima, OH 45801
- Phone: 419-222-9426
- Web Site: www.allencountymuseum.org

One of the feature attractions of this popular museum is the John Dillinger/Sherrif Sarber exhibit. The Dillinger/Sarber collection includes Dillinger's jail cell and Sarber's desk, wax figure replicas and a video documentary. The main museum covers everything from A to Z. Also on the premises are a Children's Museum and Children's Garden where kids have the opportunity to do some hands-on learning. There's an 1893 Victorian home and out-cabin open for tours, as well as a railroad collection containing old timetables, pictures, books, magazines and other material. Inside the main museum, visitors will have two floors of discovery. The main floor features sections depicting pioneer and 19th century life, a Noah's Ark exhibit, transportation displays, opera-house music, archives room, auditorium and library. The ground-level floor provides various sections and exhibits like the Sarber/Dillinger, old general store, firefighting, military and firearms, minerals and fossils, arts and pottery, multicultural, agricultural, woodworking and engraving, and Native American items.

ASHTABULA COUNTY HISTORY MUSEUM
Admission is FREE

- Open on during summer months on Wednesdays from Noon - 7:00 p.m. and Sundays from 1:00 p.m. - 5:00 p.m. The rest of the year it is open on Wednesdays from 10:00 a.m. - 4:00 p.m.
- Location: 5685 Lake Road in Geneva-On-The-Lake, OH

- Phone: 216-466-7337

Ashtabula County's history is captured inside an 1823 farm-house on the shore of Lake Erie. Visitors may tour the Victorian-style furnished rooms. In addition, the Ashtabula County Historical Society maintains the 1810 Blakeslee Log Cabin, which is located at 441 Seven Hills Road in Ashtabula city. It is open by appointment.

AURORA HISTORICAL SOCIETY MUSEUM
Admission is FREE

- Open Tuesdays and Thursdays from 1:00 p.m. - 4:00 p.m.
- Location: Aurora Memorial Library Building on East Pioneer Trail in Aurora, OH
- Phone: 216-562-8131

Say "cheese!" And pose in front of a giant cheese-making apparatus on display at the museum. The museum also features several interesting maps of the area dating back to the original map of 1799. It also features maps of the Western Reserve and the township in the 1870s. Additional items for viewing include old tools, fabrics and clothes, household items, toys, old photographs and currency (The Harmon Stone) actually issued for the region during the Civil War.

BEDFORD HISTORICAL SOCIETY MUSEUM
Admission is FREE

- Open Mondays and Wednesdyas from 7:30 a.m. - 10:00 p.m; Thursdays from 10:00 a.m. - 4:00 p.m. And the second Sunday of each month from 2:00 p.m. - 5:00 p.m.
- Location: Bedford, OH
- Phone; 440-232-0796

97

The museum is located in the restored 1874 town hall of Bedford. Come and read the diaries of pioneer women or other correspondence, speeches and manuscripts ranging from the 1850s through the 1950s. It also has a vast reference library documenting genealogical resources. Many of the areas most notable women in history are also represented by a newspaper clipping file featuring Halle Berry - Actress, a renowned criminologist, and community activist to name a few. Rotating exhibits have featured period furniture displays, military artifacts, old household tools, china collections and more.

BLACK RIVER HISTORICAL MUSEUM
Admission is FREE

- Open Sundays and Wednesdyas from 1:00 p.m. - 4:00 p.m. and Fridays from 10:00 a.m. - 1:00 p.m.
- Location: 309 West 5th St. · Lorain, OH 44052
- Phone: 440-245-2563

Visitors will see history illustrated from the early nineteenth century through the twentieth century. Its many displays and exhibits feature items such as maps, clocks, time saving devices, tools, clothing, toys, jewelry, photographs, historical documents and many other artifacts of local interest.

CUYAHOGA VALLEY HISTORICAL MUSEUM
Admission is FREE

- Open Fridays through Sundays and on Wednesdays from Noon - 4:00 p.m.
- Location: 1775 Main Street · Peninsula, OH
- Phone: 330-657-2892

Feature exhibits showcase the history of the Cuyahoga Valley. It has many historic maps, documents, photographs and other pieces on display. The museum itself is located inside the restored Boston Township Hall. The building was originally built in 1887 as a high school. And it looks its part.

FORT AMANDA
Admission is FREE

- Open daily during daylight hours
- Location: Approximately 10 miles northwest of Wapakoneta, OH along the Auglaize River
- Phone: 800-283-8713

What was war like in 1812? To find out, visit this fort and read the diary of Ohio militiaman Ensign William Schillinger, which provides a daily account from everything like the weather, events unfolding and personal thoughts and other observations. The fort itself served as an important supply depot during the War of 1812. It included five blockhouses, cabins and storage buildings. The walls of the fort were nearly 12-feet above ground.

FORT JEFFERSON
Admission is FREE

- Open daily during daylight hours
- Location: Fort Jefferson, OH near Greenville, Ohio at County Road 24 and State Route 121
- Phone: 800-686-1535

Built in 1791, this fort served as an outpost to General Arthur St. Clair. Its purpose was to shelter army supplies and guard against area Indians. It was abandoned in 1796, and is now a park with a monument, twenty-feet high, marking the site where it once stood. However, nothing of the fort remains here.

GNADUNHUTTEN MONUMENT AND MUSEUM
Admission is FREE

- Open daily between Memorial Day and Labor Day and weekends in September and October
- Location: Gnadenhutten, OH
- Phone: 614-254-4143 or 740-254-4143

This is the oldest settlement in Ohio. It was established in 1772 by a Mohican elder and large group of Christian Indians. In 1782, nearly 100 of the Indian residents were killed. Today, a 35-foot memorial recognizes those killed in the massacre. And a museum displays artifacts and an expansive arrowhead collection. There is also a reconstructed church and log cabin replications of those that stood at the site more than 200 years ago.

KNOX COUNTY HISTORICAL MUSEUM
Admission is FREE

- Open from February through Christmas on Wednesdays from 6:00 p.m. - 8:00 p.m. And Thursdays through Sundays from 2:00 p.m. - 4:00 p.m.
- Location: 875 Harcourt Road · Mount Vernon, OH 43050
- Phone: 740-393-5247
- Web Site: http://www.visitknoxohio.org/?article=museums

This historical museum features the George Tanner Telephone History Collection, the C&G Cooper Heritage Collection of 19th century steam farm engines and "Spanning the Century" exhibit of bridges. The displays throughout the museum also pay homage to the musical history of Knox County and the life and travels of Johnny Appleseed throughout the county. In addition, there are plenty of other exhibits including those of dolls, toys, textiles and clothing, coverlets and quilts among many other items.

LAKE ERIE ISLAND MUSEUM
Admission is FREE

- Call for hours
- Location: South Bass Island · Put-in-Bay, OH 43456
- Phone: 419-285-2804
- Web Site: www.leihs.org

Okay, so getting to the island may not be free unless you have a boat or can swim. The latter is not advisable and the Coast Guard may have a problem with it. Alas, once you're on the island, visit this museum and take the time to see the video history. The museum features winemaking displays, a model ship collection of historic Great Lakes' vessels, Boat Building and the Wildlife Building.

LAWRENCE COUNTY MUSEUM
Admission is FREE

- Open April through December Fridays through Sundays from 1:00 p.m. -5:00 p.m.
- Location: 506 South 6th Street · Irontown, OH 45638
- Phone: 740-532-1222

This local history museum features a permanent collection, as well as rotating exhibits year-round. It features items forging the iron-history of the region, as well as Victorian era clothing and furniture displays. The museum itself is housed in a restored 1870 Victorian home that once served to protect runaway slaves traveling the Underground Railroad.

MAHLER MUSEUM
Admission is FREE

- Open May - December on Sundays and Tuesdays from 2:00 p.m. - 4:00 p.m.
- Location: 118 East Bridge St. · Berea, OH 44017

• Phone: 440-243-2541

This museum concentrates primarily on the local history of its women citizens from the 1800's well into the 20th century. It documents the role of women as community activists and provides records from 1882 to 1936. It also documents the reading habits and ideas that influenced women in the 20th century, as well as a collection of books written by local authors.

MASSILLON MUSEUM
Admission is FREE

• Open Tuesdays - Saturdays from 9:30 a.m. - 5:00 p.m. and Sundays from 2:00 p.m. - 5:00 p.m.
• Location: 121 Lincoln Way East · Massillon, OH 44646
• Phone: 330-833-4061

If you missed the circus, come to this museum and see a room filled with circus memorabilia. Local history and its many artifacts are found in this museum as well. The museum itself is located in the former Stark Dry Goods building, which was renovated to house the museum and its belongings. It hosts various traveling exhibits and has three floors of displays, a café and gift shop.

MERCER COUNTY HISTORICAL MUSEUM
Admission is FREE

• Open October through April Wednesdays - Fridays from 8:30 a.m. - 4:00 p.m.
• Location: 130 East Market St. · Celina, OH
• Phone: 419-586-6065

200 years of county life captured in one museum. It features many books depicting local history and genealogical materials as well. The museum itself is a historic home known as the

Riley Home. And of course it has dated displays to portray the home's history and times.

OLD COURTHOUSE MUSEUM
Admission is FREE

- Open Tuesdays through Fridays from 10:00 a.m. - 4:30 p.m. and Saturdays from Noon - 4:00 p.m.
- Location: 7 N. Main St. · Dayton, OH
- Phone: 513-228-6271

Exhibits are displayed by the Montgomery County Historical Society and feature the areas history. The museum features items from the Wright Brothers to the National Cash Register Company and its founder - John Patterson. This old courthouse and the courthouse square have been witness to speeches by Presidents from Lincoln to Reagan. As a national historical monument, the structure is one of the finest Classical revivals in the country.

PERRY HISTORICAL MUSEUM
Admission is FREE

- Open to the public on the second Saturday of each month from Noon - 4:00 p.m.
- Location: Center Road and Main Street intersection in Perry, OH
- Phone: 440-259-4541

The museum once served as the original Perry town hall. It was built in 1875. The museum displays many historic photographs, documents and memoirs. It also features letters, furniture, clothing, collectibles and other relics covering the region's historic roots.

PORTAGE COUNTY HISTORICAL SOCIETY
Admission is FREE

- Open Sundays, Tuesdays and Thursdays from 2:00 p.m. - 4:00 p.m.
- Location: 6549 North Chestnut St. · Ravenna, OH 44266
- Phone: 330-296-3523
- Web Site: www.history.portage.oh.us/museum.html

The 12-acre museum site includes the John Lowrie & Mary Helen Beatty Museum, a pioneer homestead, land grant office, 1810 New England barn, Ford Seed Company museum, steam traction engine and a distinctive clock tower with an 1882 clock and bell. The museum itself has a vast collection of artifacts including Native-American tools, pottery, casting tools, Riddle Hearse, military items, farm tools, saddles, household fixtures, kids clothes and toys, and women's clothing and jewelry. Visitors should be sure to see the cathedral style stained glass window, which originally came from the courthouse built in 1882.

ROMBACH PLACE:
CLINTON COUNTY HISTORICAL SOCIETY
Admission is FREE

- Open March through December Wednesdays through Fridays from 1:00 p.m. - 4:00 p.m.
- Location: 149 East Locust St. · Wilmington, OH 45177
- Phone: 937-382-4684
- Web Site: www.clintoncountyhistory.org

The museum highlights General James W. Denver (for whom Denver, Colorado was named), Eli Harvey (artist and sculptor), and Carl Moon (photographer of the Southwest). James Denver moved to Wilmington, Ohio in 1831. His personal library and military artifacts are on display. Eli Harvey was an internationally known artist. His works are on display. And Carl Moon's photos of Southwest Indians are on display. He was one of the first to photograph Native-Americans in their traditional environment and culture. The museum's Quaker Room is dedicated to items demonstrating the simple living of Clinton County's earlier settlers. In addition, there are many Victorian artifacts, furniture and clothing to see as well.

SHAKER HISTORICAL MUSEUM
Admission is FREE

- Open Tuesdays, Wednesdays, Thursdays, Fridays and Sundays from 2:00 p.m. - 5:00 p.m.
- Location: 16740 South Park Boulevard · Shaker Heights, OH 44120
- Phone: 216-921-1201
- Web Site: http://www.cwru.edu/affil/shakhist/one.htm

The museum is located inside a huge old mansion and features displays of shaker furniture and artifacts. It also exhibits many other items from the original shaker community, which was founded in 1822. It's main business was selling hand-made furniture. The shakers were known for their simplicity in life style.

STRONGSVILLE HISTORICAL SOCIETY VILLAGE
Admission is FREE

- Open April through November on Wednesdays, Saturdays and Sundays from 1:00 p.m. - 4:00 p.m.
- Location: 13305 Pearl Rd. · Strongsville, OH
- Phone: 440-238-0057
- Web Site: http://www.strongsville.org/html/historical_society.html

See what it was like to stroll through a nineteenth century village complete with a general store. Additional buildings include a log cabin and millinery. All of the buildings that are at this quaint little recreated village are either original structures in their original places or original structures moved to the village from other locations throughout Strongsville.

VAN WERT COUNTY HISTORICAL MUSEUM
Admission is FREE

- Open March through December on Sundays from 2:00 p.m. - 4:30 p.m.
- Location: 602 N. Washington St. · Van Wert, OH 45891
- Phone: 419-238-5297
- Web Site: http://www.geocities.com/vanwertmuseum/

What's not to see at this local treasure? The museum is inside an 1896 Victorian home and has many displays covering virtually every period in Van Wert history, including its Native-American ancestor age. In addition to Indian artifacts, exhibits include old pictures of the town and memorabilia regarding its military involvements. Other attractions feature a 1951 Pennsylvania Railroad caboose, one-room schoolhouse built in 1906, a large barn and 1860 log cabin home.

ADDITIONAL HISTORY MUSEUMS

Moreland Hills Historical Society Museum
Admission is FREE

- Open Mondays through Fridays from 8:30 a.m. - 4:30 p.m.
- Location: Village Hall · 4350 SOM Center Road · Moreland Hills, OH

- Phone: 440-247-7282

The museum is housed in a renovated old schoolhouse and features memorabilia from President James A. Garfield.

Solon Historical Museum
Admission is FREE

- Open from 1:00 p.m. - 4:00 p.m. on the second Wednesday of each month only
- Location: 33975 Bainbridge Rd. · Solon, OH.
- Phone: 440-248-6419

This local history museum exhibits memorabilia of the Solon are history.

Maple Heights Historical Museum
Admission is FREE

- Open Mondays and Wednesdays from 7:00 p.m. - 9:00 p.m. the second Sunday of each month from 1:00 p.m. - 4:00 p.m. between June and September.
- Location: Maple Heights, OH
- Phone: 216-662-2851

Formerly a one-room schoolhouse, this museum exhibits, primarily, historic photographs and old household items used by early-day residents.

Shelby Museum of History
Admission is FREE

- Open May through October on Sundays from 2:00 p.m. - 5:00 p.m. (Closed on Mothers' Day and Fathers' Day)
- Location: 76 Raymond Avenue · Shelby, OH 44875
- Web Site: www.rootsweb.com/~ohscogs/ shelbymuseum/1.html

The Shelby museum is home to a wide-array of artifacts and memorabilia illustrating the history of Shelby, Ohio and its businesses and citizens.

Lakewood Historical Society
Admission is FREE

- Open on Wednesdays from 1:00 p.m. - 4:00 p.m. and on Sundays from 2:00 p.m. - 5:00 p.m.
- Location: 14710 Lake Avenue · Lakewood, OH.
- Phone: 216-221-7343

Lakewood's history is on display representing the life and times of the community's past and present.

Seneca County Museum
Admission is FREE

- Call for hours.
- Location: 28 Clay St. · Tiffin, OH.
- Phone: 419-447-5955

The museum is located inside a Greek Revival historical house built in 1853. Among its collection of Seneca County memorabilia, it also features rooms concentrating on the Tiffin glass industry's history and a carriage house displaying antique fire-fighting equipment and horse-drawn carriages.

Euclid Historical Museum
Admission is FREE

- Open Tuesdays through Sundays from 1:00 p.m. - 4:00 p.m.
- Location: 21129 North St. · Euclid, OH.
- Phone: 216-289-8577

This museum displays early Western Reserve artifacts and other relics depicting the history of the Euclid area community.

Ottawa County Historical Museum
Admission is FREE

- Call for hours
- Location: 126 West Third Street · Port Clinton, OH
- Phone: 419-732-2337

Memorabilia representing the area's history includes fossils, linens, dolls and Native-American artifacts and arrowheads. It also has displays depicting the local community and military history.

Brooklyn Historical Society
Admission is FREE

- Open Tuesdays from 10:00 a.m. - 2:00 p.m. and Sundays from 2:00 p.m. - 5:00 p.m.
- Location: 4442 Ridge Road · Brooklyn, OH.
- Phone: 216-749-2804

The Brooklyn museum features artifacts of furniture dating between 1830 and the 1950's.

Garfield Heights Historical Museum
Admission is FREE

- Open on Saturdays from 1:00 p.m. - 4:00 p.m.
- Location: 5405 Turney Rd. · Garfield Heights, OH
- Phone: 216-475-3050

The museum is housed in a century home with a herb garden just outside.

IF YOU BUILD IT, THEY WILL COME
(Homes, Castles & Farms)

And if you build it well enough, they will come for generations. At least that's the case with many of the historic homes, mansions, castles, and farms found herein.

About those farms: Have you ever been to a fish-petting farm? Or, have you been down on the farm - as in Bob Evans' original homestead?

Well, they built it, now it's time for you to go see it.

AGRICULTURE MUSEUM AND VILLAGE
Admission is FREE

- Open between June and August on Sundays from 1:00 p.m. - 4:00 p.m.
- Location: Hardin County east of the fairgrounds off of Route-140
- Phone: 419-673-7147

This turn-of-the-century farmstead features many farming instruments and pioneer architecture. Highlights of the museum/village include the Stadt Log House and Dunkirk Jailhouse.

BOB EVAN'S FARM
Admission is FREE (Fee for additional activities)

- Open Memorial Day to Labor Day and on Weekends in September from 8:30 a.m. - 5:00 p.m.
- Location: State Route 588 · Rio Grande, OH
- Phone: 800-994-FARM
- Web Site: www.bobevans.com

Make your pilgrimage to where it all began "down on the farm." Yes, the original 1,000 acre Bob Evans farm, including dozens of horses and more than 100 cattle. Begin your tour with Bob's first restaurant named, The Sausage Shoppe, and continue to the farm museum, log cabin village, one-room schoolhouse, small animal barnyard, craft barn, stage coach and much more. For a fee, you can also take part in canoe trips, overnight horse trail rides and many weekend events such as the annual Bob Evans Farm Festival. The "Homestead" is listed on the National Register of Historic Places and is where Bob and his wife, Jewell, raised their six children. It used to be a stagecoach stop and inn.

CARRIAGE HILL FARM AND MUSEUM
Admission is FREE

- Open weekdays 10:00 a.m. - 5:00 p.m. and weekends from 1:00 p.m. - 5:00 p.m. Location: East Shull Road & Route 201, Huber Heights, OH
- Phone: 937-879-0461
- Web Site: http://www.metroparks.org/Facilities/ Carriage_Hill_MetroPark/carriage_hill_metropark.html

Carriage Hill Farm and Museum are part of the Dayton Metro Parks. Visitors will see what it was like to work on a farm in the 1880's. It has restored buildings that include a blacksmith shop, summer kitchen, woodshop and barns with a variety of animals. There are also hands-on displays for children. Household chores and farming are demonstrated as they were more than 100 years ago. While you're there, don't miss the scenic views of woodlands, meadows, lake and pond.

CATHEDRAL BASILICA OF
THE ASSUMPTION
Admission is FREE

- Open Tuesdays through Sundays from 10:00 a.m. - 4:00 p.m.
- Location: 1140 Madison Avenue (near downtown Cincinnati, OH) in Covington, KY
- Phone: 859-431-2060

See the largest stained glass window in the world and only one of 31 basilicas in the U.S. The window measures 67 feet by 24 feet. The cathedral also touches the senses with more than 80 additional stained glass windows and its French Gothic design, complete with gargoyles and flying buttresses.

CHRISTMAS MANOR
Admission is Free

- Open from the last weekend in September through December 23 on Mondays - Saturdays from 10:00 a.m. - 9:00 p.m. and Sundays from Noon - 5:00 p.m. (Also, open Thanksgiving Day from 3:00 p.m. - 8:00 p.m.)
- Location: Bryan, OH
- Phone: 419-636-3082
- Web Site: www.christmasmanor.com

We invite you to pay a visit to Christmas Manor, a nineteen room, circa 1874 Victorian Italianate home (located in Bryan, Ohio). This is one of N.W. Ohio's most visited attractions. Thousands of gifts and decorations are displayed throughout this magnificent home. The decorating ideas you see can easily be transferred to any home. So come catch the spirit of Christmas at Christmas Manor. During the off season, visit the Christmas Manor "Home for the Holidays-Gift Shop" & "Fireside Books." It is open with limited hours. Gifts are displayed in a cozy home atmosphere.

FOLLETT HOUSE MUSEUM
Admission is FREE

- Open April, May, September, October, November and December on Saturdays and Sundays from Noon - 4:00 p.m. and June, July and August on Tuesdays through Saturdays from Noon - 4:00 p.m. Closed January, February and March
- Location: 404 Wayne Street · Sandusky, OH 44870
- Phone: 419-627-9608
- Web Site: www.sandusky.lib.oh.us/follett_house.html

The Follett House Museum has an extensive collection of archival materials chronicling the Sandusky and Erie County region. It includes several artifacts from the Underground Railroad. The museum is a branch of the Sandusky Library. The 1827 mansion was built by Oran Follett in Greek-Revival style. Follett was a businessman and one of the founders of the Republican Party. The museum's Civil War collection includes items from the Confederate officers' prison on Johnson Island. Other fine artifacts in the museum's possession are diaries, letters, drawings and photographs from the Johnson Island Prison. It also displays books, maps and manuscripts. When you visit, take in the panoramic view of Sandusky, Cedar Point and Johnson's Island from the mansion's widow's walk. The Follett House Museum is listed in the National Register of Historic Landmarks.

FRANZEE HOUSE
Admission is FREE

- Open April through October on Saturdays and Sundays from 10:00 a.m. - 5:00 p.m.
- Location: 7733 Canal Road · Peninsula, OH 44141
- Phone: 216-524-1497

Built in the mid 1820s during the time of the construction of the northern portion of the Ohio and Erie Canals, this home exhibits excellent examples of Western Reserve architectural style and construction techniques used at the time.

FRESHWATER FARMS OF OHIO
FREE Tour

- Open by appointment only. A tour is best scheduled in the morning during the early part of the week.
- Location: 2624 North U.S. Highway 68 · Urbana, OH 43078
- Phone: 800-634-7434
- Web Site: www.fwfarms.com

Have you ever pet a Sturgeon fish? Do you want to? Well, if so, Freshwater Farms of Ohio is the place to do it. In addition, you will learn how the largest indoor fish farm in Ohio started. Visitors may feed the fish in all-weather outdoor tanks and see their "guard" cat. This family-operated farm is a leader in the aquaculture industry and provides fresh farm-raised Rainbow trout, yellow perch, and other fish hatched from eggs in a solar-heated hatchery.

FROSTVILLE MUSEUM
Admission is FREE

- Open Memorial Day through October on Sundays from 2:00 p.m. - 5:00 p.m.
- Location: 24101 Cedar Point Rd. · Rocky River Reservation · Olmsted Falls, OH 44138
- Phone: 440-884-8844
- Web Site: http://www.n2net.net/members/mgrogan/

The Frostville Museum highlights the local 19th Century history and features several landmarks. The Brigg's Homestead built in 1836, the Jenkin's Cabin built in the early 1800s, the John Carpenter House built in 1840, and the Prechtel House built in 1874 are some of the featured buildings at this site. Each structure displays museum items that reflect the day and times of pioneer life, rural Victorian American life and other historic artifacts.

GRANT'S BOYHOOD HOME & SCHOOLHOUSE
Admission is FREE

- Call for appointment
- Location: Georgetown, OH
- Phone: 937-378-4222

See the humble beginnings of Ulysses S. Grant. This is where the great Civil War general and President of the United States lived and learned from approximately six - thirteen years of age. The schoolhouse was originally a one-room structure built in 1829. And the home is a restored white colonial. Grant, 1839-1865, was born in Mount Pleasant, Ohio.

HARRIET BEECHER STOWE HOUSE
Admission is FREE

- Open Tuesdays, Wednesdays and Thursdays from 10:00 a.m. - 4:00 p.m.
- Location: 2950 Gilbert Avenue (State Route 3, U.S. 22) Cincinnati, OH 45214
- Phone: 513-632-5120
- Web Site: www.ohiohistory.org/places/stowe

Harriet Beecher Stowe is the author of Uncle Tom's Cabin. Stowe was inspired to write this historic book when she learned of the evils of slavery. Built in 1833 by Lane Seminary, the Harriet Beecher Stowe House served as the residence for the institution's president. In 1832, Harriet Beecher moved to Cincinnati from Connecticut with her father, Dr. Lyman Beecher who was appointed president of the seminary.

HUBBARD HOUSE
Admission is FREE

- Open Memorial Day through August on Fridays, Saturdays and Sundays from Noon - 6:00 p.m. (September and October from 1:00 p.m. - 5:00 p.m.)
- Location: Corner of Walnut Blvd. And Lake Ave. in Ashtabula, OH 44004
- Phone: 440-964-8168

Once a stop along the Underground Railroad, this 1840's house was built by William and Catherine Hubbard and served as a refuge for escaped slaves. Its displays include old maps and photographs and Civil War items. It is furnished according to the appropriate period and style to reflect the homes history. The home itself is listed in the Department of Interior's National Historic Register.

JOHN SMART HOUSE
Admission is FREE

- Open Tuesdays and Thursdays from 9:30 a.m. - 5:30 p.m. and on the first Sunday of each month from 1:00 p.m. - 4:00 p.m. Closed January and February.
- Location: 206 N. Elmwood · Medina, OH 44258
- Phone: 330-722-1341

At the John Smart House, you will see what life during the Victorian era was like. Beautiful furnishings, exhibits and vintage clothing are displayed. You will also enjoy pioneer artifacts, Civil War pieces, Native-American tools (including arrowhead displays). On an interesting note, see life-sized pictures, boots and helmet of real-life giants - Martin and Anna Bates.

LANE HOOVEN HOUSE
Admission is FREE

- Open Mondays through Fridays from 9:00 a.m. - 4:00 p.m.
- Location: 319 N. 3rd St. · Hamilton, OH 45011
- Phone: 513-863-1389

The Lane Hooven House was built in 1863 by industrialist Clark Lane and later restored. This octagonal Gothic Revival style brick home has a unique spiral staircase running up to the third-floor turret, a stain-glass entrance and some period furnishings throughout. The main floor is enriched with butternut and ash woodwork.

LOG HOUSE MUSEUM
Admission is FREE

- Open June, July and August on Saturdays and Sundays from 2:00 p.m. - 4:00 p.m. Closed holidays
- Location: 10 East Park Avenue · Columbiana, OH 44408

The Log House Museum was built in the 1820s by Jacob Nessly and is now used by The Historical Society of Columbiana-Fairfield Township. The museum features quilts and coverlets from the 1830s, pioneer items and on a more interesting note: a set of 10,000 year-old Mastodon bones found by a nearby farm. Also, you will see Civil War artifacts and more. Please note that photos are allowed, even with a flash. You can park for free on an adjacent church property.

THE MANOR HOUSE
Admission is FREE

- Open Wednesday through Sunday from Noon - 5:00 p.m.
- Location: Wildwood Preserve Metroparks in Toledo, OH
- Phone: 419-535-3050
- Web Site: www.metroparkstoledo.com/manor.html

This Georgian colonial mansion was built in 1938 for Robert Stranahan, cofounder of the Champion Spark Plug Company. The Manor House has 35 primary rooms, 17 bathrooms and 16 fireplaces. Most of the rooms are refurbished with period appropriate pieces. The estate grounds also have the former riding stables, limousine garage and symmetrical formal gardens next to brick walls with wrought iron gazebos.

MCGUFFEY MUSEUM
Admission is FREE

- Open Saturdays and Sundays from Noon - 4:00 p.m. (Closed in August)
- Location: Miami University · Oxford, OH 45056
- Phone: 513-529-2232
- Web Site: http://www.lib.muohio.edu/mcguffey/ museum.php

This was the home of William Holmes McGuffey, professor of Ancient Languages and Moral Philosophy at Miami University from 1826 - 1836, and is now registered as a National Historic Landmark. The museum/home honors McGuffey and his Eclectic Readers, which were a series of books that educated five generations of Americans and are said to be the most widely published books in the U.S. except for the Holy Bible.

MILLIONAIRES ROW
FREE Self-guided Tour

- Location: Euclid Avenue near downtown Cleveland, OH
- Web Site: http://www.ohiopreservation.org/euclid.htm

What was once know as "the most beautiful street in America" is now a distant memory more than a century later. Cleveland's Euclid Avenue, otherwise known as Millionaires Row, was once the residential street of some of the most influential families in American history and their lavish estates. These monstrous mansions with broad sweeping lawns, ornate architecture and wondrous landscapes used to be home to industrial tycoons and celebrated philanthropists like Rockefeller, Mather, Wade, Severance, Gund, Stone, Brush and Everett, and political figures such as John Hay, Tom Johnson and Leonard Hanna. Now, only 10 homes remain on the once famed avenue. And most of those are hidden from view by the byproduct of their industrial architects - buildings. However, you can still take a stroll down memory lane and see what's left but do so at your own risk because this isn't exactly Rockefeller's neighborhood anymore. The homes that remain in whole or in part include the following:

1. Luther Allen House (7609 Euclid Avenue)
2. Morris Bradley Carriage House (7217 Euclid Avenue)
3. John Henry Devereaux (3226 Euclid Avenue)
4. Francis Drury House (8625 Euclid Avenue)
5. Hall-Sullivan House (7218 Euclid Avenue)
6. Howe Residence (2248 Euclid Avenue)
7. Samuel Mather Residence (2605 Euclid Avenue)
8. Stager-Beckwith House (3813 Euclid Avenue)
9. Lyman Treadway House (8917 Euclid Avenue)
10. H.W. White Residence (8937 Euclid Avenue)

These homes were once stunning monuments to America's growing prosperity. Those remaining sit like relics releasing a hint of what was once "the most beautiful street in America."

OLD STONE HOUSE MUSEUM
Admission is FREE (Donations welcome)

• Open Sundays from 2:00 p.m. - 5:00 p.m; Wednesdays from 1:00 p.m. - 4:00 p.m. Closed December and January as well as major holidays
• Location: 14710 Lake Avenue · Lakewood, OH
• Phone: 216-221-7374
• Web Site: www.lkwdpl.org/histsoc/

This 1838 "old stone house" was originally the residence of a Scottish immigrant and later served as a post office, shoe repair shop, grocery store, doctors office and barber shop. Now, as a museum, it provides a look at the city's pioneer past with displays of furniture, household items, clothing, tools, books, toys, dolls and a spinning wheel. The home comes complete with a sickroom with old-fashioned equipment to care for the ill. Also on display are roped beds, cooking fireplace, four-harness loom, furnished parlor, handmade linens and more. The Old Stone House has a cousin linked to it - Nicholson House. This 1835 home is an example of early Western Reserve architecture. Both homes are listed in the National Register of Historic Places.

ROBBINS-HUNTER MUSEUM
Admission is FREE

- Open Wednesdays through Sundays from 1:00 p.m. - 4:00 p.m.
- Location: 221 E. Broadway · Granville, OH
- Phone: 740-587-0430
- Web Site: www.lickingcountyhistoricalsociety.org

This museum house was built in 1842 and has 27 rooms. The rooms are furnished with 18th and 19th century American and European furniture, decorative arts, paintings and sculptures. Robbins Hunter once operated an antique business from this home. Other displays within the museum include, oriental rugs, antique clocks, china and silver.

ROSE HILL MUSEUM
Admission is FREE

- Open Sundays from 2:00 p.m. - 4:30 p.m. only.
- Location: 27715 Lake Road · Bay Village, OH 44140
- Phone: 440-871-7338
- Web Site: http://www.victoriana.com/bvhs/ museum.html

This museum-home was built in 1818 as a private residence and once served as the town's library. The three-story structure has furnishings from the Colonial and Victorian periods. The grounds also house a cabin replica and Smoke House.

SHERWOOD-DAVIDSON HOUSE MUSEUM
Admission is FREE

- Open Tuesdays through Sundays from 1:00 p.m. - 4:00 p.m. Closed January through March.
- Location: 6 N. 6 St. · Newark, OH 43055
- Phone: 740-345-6525
- Web Site: www.lickingcountyhistoricalsociety.org

Built in 1815, The Sherwood-Davidson House is an example of Federal architecture. You enter the home through a front-fanned doorway. It has a two-story side gallery, portable wooden and tin shower built before 1860, and a kitchen with a collection of pioneer utensils. It is furnished with Victorian furnishings.

SLATE RUN HISTORICAL FARM
Admission is FREE

- Call for hours.
- Location: 9130 Marcy Road · Ashville, OH (Operated by Columbus Metroparks)
- Phone: 614-833-1880
- Web Site: http://www.metroparks.co.franklin.oh.us/ slaterun.htm

Hey kids, are you afraid to get your hands dirty? I didn't think so. Well, roll up your sleeves and join in the farm life - 1800's style - at Slate Run Historical Farm. It's in full operation year-round as a living historical farm, not just a museum. Chores change with the seasons just like real-life and the staff dresses the part of the times. So, step-back into early farm and family life and watch chores carried out with the tools, equipment and methods used in the old-fashioned days without electricity and other modern conveniences. It's the perfect cure for kids that won't clean their rooms.

SQUIRE'S CASTLE
Admission is FREE

- Open from Dawn - Dusk.
- Location: Willoughby Hills, OH Metropark
- Phone: 440-526-7165

This stone building known as Squire's Castle" isn't really a castle at all. Rather, it is the caretakers house for a lavish mansion that was never built. The stone castle-like home was built in the 1890s by Feargus Squire, one of the founders of Standard Oil Company. He had planned a summer estate in the Cleveland countryside. His plans changed when his wife died. And the mansion never left the drawing board. However, the Squire Castle is still a nice place to visit although it has been stripped of its glass windows, interior walls, furnishings, and even had the basement filled for fear of vandals. Still, wandering this stone home is interesting. It will leave the mind to wonder what if... Bring a picnic basket and spend the afternoon in the forest by this century old architectural dream.

STEARNS HOMESTEAD
Admission is FREE

- Open June through October on Saturdays and Sundays from 1:00 p.m. - 4:30 p.m.
- Location: 6975 Ridge Road · Parma, OH
- Phone: 440-845-9770

This 48-acre historical farm includes the 1855 Stearns House, 1920 Gibbs House, country store, meeting cabin, out buildings, barn and farm animals. Both of the houses are museums with period appropriate displays and furnishings. In addition, visitors will see an 1848 fire engine and more.

SULLIVAN - JOHNSON MUSEUM
Admission is FREE

- Open Saturdays and Sundays from 1:00 p.m. - 4:00 p.m.
- Location: 223 N. Main St. in Kenton, OH
- Phone: 419-673-7147

This 1896 mansion serves as a historical museum featuring early settler and Native-American items amongst other memorabilia from some of Kenton's most notable residents.

TALLMADGE CHURCH
Admission is FREE

- Open year-round.
- Location: Public Circle in Tallmadge, OH 44278
- Phone: 330-733-5879

This architectural landmark was once featured in the November 20, 1944 issue of Life Magazine. It was designed by a seven-member committee in 1819 and built in 1822. The appointed architect and builder of the church was Lemuel Porter. The wood church was designed in a Greek Revival portico. Its main features include four large columns and a steeple with a weathervane standing one hundred feet high.

TELLING MANSION
Admission is FREE

- Open Saturdays from 1:00 p.m. - 4:00 p.m.
- Location: 4645 Mayfield Road · South Euclid, OH
- Phone: 216-691-0314

This five-room mansion comes with a Victorian parlor. Currently, it is home to a branch of the Cuyahoga Community Library and South Euclid Historical Society Museum. It was built in 1928 and is now listed on the National Register of Historic Places. It is a French-style chateau.

THE 1810 HOUSE
Admission is FREE

- Open from May through November on Saturdays and Sundays from 2:00 p.m. - 4:00 p.m. Also, open in December for a special Christmas display and other times by appointment
- Location: 1926 Waller Street · Portsmouth, OH
- Phone: 740-354-3760

This former two-story brick farm homestead turned museum houses many pioneer artifacts. There are eight rooms that visitors may tour and view 19th and 20th century furnishings, house-wares and clothing. See what families did in their living rooms for activities and entertainment, as well as what sort of items children of the time used to play. Teachers will want to see the Old Schoolroom and its desks, books and teaching tools of the past. The kitchen is well stocked with china, utensils and more, including a cast iron stove.

THURBER HOUSE
Admission is FREE

- Open daily from Noon - 4:00 p.m.
- Location: 77 Jefferson Avenue · Columbus, OH 43215
- Phone: 614-464-1032
- Web Site: www.thurberhouse.org/ThurberHouse.htm

The Thurber House is a restored nineteenth-century home where author, humorist, cartoonist, and playwright James Thurber lived during his college days with his parents. Thurber used this home's characteristics in many of his stories. The home has since been restored to represent the early teens of the 20th century. And of course, visitors will see Thurber memorabilia, including original drawings, manuscripts and first editions of his books. In addition, his typewriter, briefcase, family photographs and more are on display.

TOLEDO'S HISTORIC OLD WEST END
FREE self-guided tour

- Location: Toledo, OH
- Web Site: www.oldwestendtoledo.com

The Old West End of Toledo, Ohio is a vintage neighborhood that features one of the oldest and largest collection of Victorian and Edwardian homes in the nation. Visit Toledo and take a walk through this well kept time capsule that showcases a myriad of architectural beauty. The homes are found at the following addresses:

- The Edward Drummond Libbey House (2008 Scottwood)
- The Julius G. Lamson House (2056 Scottwood)
- John Barber Home (2271 Scottwood)
- Moses G. Block House (2272 Scottwood)
- The Wright - Wilmington House (2320 Scottwood)

- Edward F. Brucker House (2055 Robinwood)
- Michael Henahan House (2052 Robinwood)
- Albin B. Tillighast House (2210 Robinwood)
- Frederick O. Paddock House (2233 Robinwood)
- The Julius H. Tyler House (2251 Robinwood)
- The William H. Currier House (2611 Robinwood)
- The Stranahan-Rothschild House (2104 Parkwood)
- The Leeper-Geddes House (2116 Parkwood)
- John Waite House (2256 Collingwood)

UNITED DAIRY FARMERS
FREE Tour

- Call for hours open
- Location: 3955 Montgomery Road · Cincinnati, OH 45212
- Phone: 513-396-8700

At this farm, visitors can weigh themselves on a giant truck scale and step inside a deep freezer room. Also, visitors can watch how ice cream is packed and frozen, and see milk filled into containers with plastic bottles made from blown pellets of plastic. If that's not enough, treat yourself to an ice cream sundae right off the production line - complimentary of course.

WEBB HOUSE MUSEUM
Admission is FREE

- Open Thursdays, Fridays and Sundays from 1:00 p.m. - 4:00 p.m. Closed January through March.
- Location: 303 Granville St. · Newark, OH 43055
- Phone: 740-345-8540
- Web Site: www.lickingcountyhistoricalsociety.org

The Webb home was built in 1907. All of its rooms are open to the public and maintain the look of a private residence. Also on the grounds are a carriage house and restored large perennial gardens.

FROM THE CRADLE TO THE GRAVE
(Famous Birthplaces & Memorials)

It's a drab title but none more true.

Famous people intrigue us - dead or alive. And we often want to learn all we can about the lives they led.

From several former Presidents of the United States and war soldiers to industrialists and ballplayers, we encourage you to explore their birthplaces, tombs and memorials.

It's time to learn about our Ohio legends - from their cradles to their graves.

BIG BOTTOM
Admission is FREE

- Open daily from Dawn - Dusk
- Location: Stockport, OH
- Phone: 614-297-2630

The Big Bottom is a memorial to commemorate a settler/Indian war, which began with a massive massacre of Ohio settler by the Delaware and Wyandot Indians in 1791. The twelve-foot marble marker has been placed here for remembrance of what happened. The bloodshed between the fighting parties went on for four years until the historic Treaty of Greenville ended it.

BUFFINGTON ISLAND MONUMENT
Admission is FREE

- Open daily from dusk - Dawn.
- Location: Meigs County on Route 124 approximately 20 miles east of Pomeroy, OH
- Phone: 800-686-1535

Don't be misled, you will not have to swim or take a ferry to see this park and monument, as it is not really located on an island. The monument is a tribute to the soldiers who fought in a major Civil War battle here in Ohio. Renowned Major Daniel McCook of the "fighting McCook" family was a casualty of the battle. The monument itself was built from broken glacial rock found in Ohio.

CAPTAIN HOOK'S TOMB
Admission is FREE

- Location: Old Brick Cemetery in Stockport, OH 43787 off State Route 376
- Phone: 740-962-5861

Captain Isaac Newton Hook (1819-1906) decided to design his own grave, according to legend, with a point on top so his wife wouldn't dance on it.

CUSTER MEMORIAL
Admission is FREE

- Open daily during daylight hours
- Location: North of Cadiz, OH in Harrison County off of State Route 646
- Phone: 740-946-3781
- Web Site: www.ohiohistory.org/places/custer

The Custer Monument is a bronze statue depicting George Armstrong Custer and is located at his birthplace, which is now a roadside park and picnic area. The only thing left of Custer's house is the foundation. An exhibit pavilion accounts Custer's life and his infamous "Last Stand."

GARFIELD BIRTH SITE AND TOMB
Admission is FREE

- Open May through September on Saturdays from 10:00 a.m. - 2:00 p.m.
- Location: Moreland Hills, OH
- Phone: 440-247-7282
- Web Site: www.morelandhills.com/historical.html

Please note that this is President James A. Garfield's birth site, not the historic site, which is in Mentor, Ohio. Here, you will see a replica memorial cabin like that which was built by Garfield's father in 1829.

Garfield's buried in Lake View Cemetery in downtown Cleveland, Ohio. It is also free to visit. His tomb is in Section 15 of the cemetery. Garfield (1831-1881) was the 20th

President of the United States and was elected to office in 1880. He was assassinated in 1881 by Charles Guiteau.

HARDING'S TOMB AND MONUMENT
Admission is FREE

- Open daily during daylight hours
- Location: Marion, OH on the corner of State Route 423 and Vernon Heights Blvd.
- Phone: 740-387-9630
- Web Site: http://www.ohiohistory.org/places/hardtomb/

President Warren G. Harding's tomb is a white, circular monument made of Georgia marble and his monument is set in 10 landscaped acres and takes the appearance of a round Greek temple. He became our 29th President (the eighth from Ohio) in 1921. He was born in 1865 and died in office in June of 1923.

HARRISON'S TOMB
Admission is FREE

- Open daily during daylight hours.
- Location: 1982 Velma Avenue · Velma, OH 43211
- Phone: 800-686-1535
- Web Site: http://www.ohiohistory.org/places/harrison/

President Benjamin Harrison's (1833 - 1901) tomb and monument are made of Bedford limestone and marble. It stands 60 feet. A visitors' terrace allows a beautiful panoramic view of the Ohio River valley. He was elected our 23rd President in 1889.

LAKE VIEW CEMETERY
Admission is FREE

- Open daily from 7:30 a.m. - 5:30 p.m.
- Location: 12316 Euclid Avenue · Cleveland, OH 44106
- Phone: 216-421-2665
- Web Site: www.lakeviewcemetery.com

This is more than your ordinary cemetery. It is considered by many to be a walk through history, a vast outdoor art museum or a horticultural paradise. In any case, it is one of the finest garden cemeteries in the country, as well as one of the most historic. It has 285 acres of land and is located in central Cleveland. It is modeled after the great garden cemeteries of Victorian England and France. It also has a picturesque dam measuring 500 feet wide and 60 feet above ground. Among its numerous points of interest and appeal, visitors will be awed by the memorials of it's more famous permanent residents such as:

- President Garfield's Tomb
- John D. Rockefeller's Monument (For younger folks, imagine someone wealthier than Bill Gates and Microsoft)
- Eliot Ness - The lawman that brought infamous mobster Al Capone to justice
- James Salisbury - Creator of the Salisbury Steak
- Ray Chapman - The only player in major league baseball history to be killed during a game by a pitched ball (Cleveland Indian)
- Charles Pinkney - A minor league baseball player killed by a pitched ball
- Carl Stokes - The first black mayor of a major city (Cleveland)
- Garrett Morgan - Inventor of the gas mask and first tri-color traffic light

- Coburn Haskell - Inventor of the modern golf ball
- Collinwood School Fire Memorial - A memorial to the 172 children and two teachers who died in the biggest school accident in U.S. history (occurring on Ash Wednesday in 1908
- And many other nationally and internationally known business and industrial tycoons, philanthropists, political powers, people of the arts and entertainment world as well as ordinary people of a wide-variety of race, ethnic and financial backgrounds.

LIMA FIREFIGHTERS MEMORIAL MUSEUM
Admission is FREE

- Location: Lincoln Park on East Elm St. · Lima, OH
- Phone: 419-221-5160

This is a local tribute honoring the brave firefighters of the area. It features vintage displays depicting their history of service to the surrounding community. Here, you'll see a horse-drawn steam pumper from the 1800's, a memorial to those who were lost in service, and of course homage paid to firefighters past and present.

MANSFIELD SOLDIERS AND SAILORS MEMORIAL BUILDING MUSEUM
Admission is FREE (donations accepted)

- Open Saturdays and Sundays from 1:00 p.m. - 4:00 p.m. or by appointment
- Location: 34 Park Avenue West · Mansfield, OH 44902
- Phone: 419-525-2491

The building was built in 1888 and is the oldest building in Richland County. It displays artifacts of the county's military, civil and natural history artifacts.

NATIONAL MCKINLEY BIRTHPLACE MEMORIAL AND MUSEUM
Admission is FREE

- Open Mondays through Thursdays from 9:00 a.m. - 8:00 p.m; Fridays and Saturdays from 9:00 a.m. - 5:30 p.m. and Sundays (September - May) from 1:00 p.m. - 5:00 p.m.
- Location: 46 N. Main St. · Niles, OH 44446
- Phone: 330-652-1704
- Web Site: http://www.mckinley.lib.oh.us/memorial.htm

President William McKinley (1843 - 1901) was the 25th President of the United States. McKinley was assassinated by a deranged anarchist. The McKinley Museum is located at the McKinley Library. The monument is made of Georgian marble and stands 232 feet by 136 feet by 38 feet. In the center of the memorial is a court of honor supported by 28 columns, and features a statue of the President. The museum contains many artifacts depicting McKinley's life and presidency.

WILLIAM HOWARD TAFT NATIONAL HISTORIC SITE
Admission is FREE

- Open daily from 8:00 a.m. - 4:00 p.m.
- Location: 2038 Auburn Avenue · Cincinnati, OH 45219
- Phone: 513-684-3262
- Web Site: www.nps.gov/wiho

President William Howard Taft (1857 - 1930) was elected the 27th President of the United States in 1909. Visitors to his birthplace and boyhood home can play with old-fashioned toys, as did the former President when he was a child. Also, visitors can play dress-up with clothes of the time.

GRAVESITES OF SOME OTHER
FAMOUS OHIOANS

- Rutherford Hayes - The 19th U.S. President is buried in Fremont, OH

- Annie Oakley - The famous woman sharpshooter is buried at Brock Cemetery outside of Greenville, OH

- Moses Fleetwood "Fleet" Walker - The first black baseball player in the major leagues (yep, even before Jackie Robinson) is buried in Union Cemetery in Steubenville, OH

- Orville and Wilbur Wright - Better known as "The Wright Brothers" are both buried at Woodland Cemetery in Dayton, OH

- Aunt Jemima (Rosie Riles) - The pancake queen is buried in Redoak, OH

- Kent State Memorial - Memorial markers for the four university students who were shot down and killed by the Ohio National Guard on May 4, 1970 during a protest. The markers are placed where each of the four died.

- Erma Bombeck - Newspaper columnist and humorist is buried at Woodland Cemetery in Dayton.

- Paul Brown - The legendary football coach of the Cleveland Browns, Cincinnati Bengals, Ohio State Buckeyes and Massillon Washington High School is buried at Rose Hill Cemetery in Massillon, OH

FUN IN THE SUN - OR RAIN OR SNOW
(The Great Outdoors)

Fun in the sun is more than just enjoying our parklands. Although that's a good place to begin, this section will take you to places you may not have known existed - until now.

Take for instance, the ancient Indian (Native-American) burial mounds or fascinating man-made structures that are withstanding the test of time. Or, the natural wonders found in Ohio, and multiple nature centers, lighthouses and covered bridges, as well as other very interesting intrastate places to take a trip. Need I go on?

Don't let the rain or snow stop you from discovering the great outdoors.

PLACES TO VISIT

This section is for various places that you can visit for free but don't exactly fit in other categories of the book. Therefore, consider them miscellaneous but make no mistake - they deserve a look.

Cleveland Metroparks Zoo
Admission is FREE for Cuyahoga County and Hinckley Township residents on Mondays ONLY. (If a legal holiday falls on a Monday, an admission is charged but the FREE day will apply on the next day - Tuesday instead)

- Open daily from 10:00 a.m. - 5:00 p.m. (extended to 7:00 p.m. during summer)
- Location: 3900 Wildlife Way · Cleveland, OH 44109
- Phone: 216-661-6500
- Web Site: www.clemetzoo.com

Ready for safari? This is no ordinary zoo. It lays claim to the largest collection of primates in North America. In addition, there are thousands of additional animals to see, hear and yes, smell throughout nearly 170 acres of discovery. The zoo also features an Australian Adventure and enormous two-acre indoor tropical rainforest. The Australian Adventure is designed for children and has many unique sites, sounds and activities available for its little explorers. And the rainforest captures the mood just right with its towering waterfall entrance and a room that rains every 15 minutes. It comes complete with wildlife, including animals and plants.

Mt. Lookout Observatory
Admission is FREE

- Open Thursdays and Fridays after dusk
- Location: 3489 Observatory Place · Cincinnati, OH 45208
- Phone: 513-321-5186

Come see the stars. And I don't mean Hollywood's. Hey, you may even make a discovery of a new planet, see a meteor or just star-gaze at the constellations. In any case, Mt. Lookout Observatory was the first professional observatory in the country.

Roscoe Village
*Admission to the village is FREE but the tour
of the inside of the buildings is NOT.*

- Open Mondays through Saturdays from 10:00 a.m. - 6:00 p.m. (Sundays until 5:00 p.m.)
- Location: 381 Hill St. · Coshocton, OH 43812
- Phone: 800-877-1830
- Web Site: www.roscoevillage.com

See what a canal town in the 1800's looked like. The buildings and people dressed as if they were right out of the once bustling port on the Erie and Ohio Canal are a site to see. This historic canal village is a nice place to spend a lazy afternoon. Visitors can mill around the town free of charge. However, tours of inside the historic buildings cost a fee. It is open year-round, although the buildings are closed in January and February.

Sorrowful Mother Shrine
Admission is FREE

- Call for hours
- Location: 4106 State Route 269 · Bellevue, OH 44811
- Phone: 419-483-3435
- Web Site: www.sanduskyfunspots.com/funspots/sms/smshome.htm

If it's spiritual reawakening you have in mind, there's a great place right here in Ohio ready for you to make a pilgrimage.

The shrine was established in 1850 as one of the first in the Midwest. It rests on 120 acres of serene and scenic land. There are paved walkways intertwined with trees leading visitors to the Stations of the Cross and replicas of Lourdes and Sepulchre Grottos. It also has many statues, memorials, additional shrines and grottos for visitors to take homage and meditate or pray. Additional highlights include the Grotto of the Tomb of Christ and Alpine Grotto/Crucifixion Scene to name a couple.

MAN-MADE AND WITHSTANDING
THE TEST OF TIME

In the name of progress, we must build and leave our mark behind. And if built well enough, it'll stay a very long time.

Buckeye Furnace
Admission is FREE

- Open from Memorial Day through Labor Day Wednesdays - Saturdays from 9:30 a.m. - 5:00 p.m. and Sundays from Noon - 5:00 p.m. (September through October open Sundays from 1:00 p.m. - 5:00 p.m.)
- Location: 123 Buckeye Park Rd. · Wellston, OH 45692
- Phone: 740-384-3537

Built in 1852, this reconstructed charcoal-fired iron blast furnace is a site to see. It includes an original stack. The site includes a reconstructed casting shed, an engine house and former company store. Furnaces such as that found here, were used for producing iron. The 270-acre park-site includes hiking trails.

Fallen Timbers
Admission is FREE

- Open daily during daylight hours

- Location: 5100 West Central Ave. · Toledo, OH 43615
- Phone: 419-535-3050

This is the historic battle site where General Anthony Wayne had a decisive victory, resulting in the Indians of the Northwest Territory signing the Treaty of Greenville. The treaty gave the southern and eastern regions of Ohio to the settlers. The name Fallen Timbers was derived due to a massive windstorm knocking down trees just before the battle. The park also has a monument honoring Wayne, the soldiers and Indians who died there.

Inscription Rock
Admission is FREE

- Open daily dawn to dusk
- Location: Kelly's Island in Lake Erie off the Port Clinton, OH shore
- Phone: 419-797-4530

Archeologists believe that these prehistoric Indian rock inscriptions date between 1200 and 1600. Much of the 32 by 21 foot rock has been eroded through time by the lake but a roof has since been built to preserve what's left, and a viewing platform was created for visitors to appreciate the remains. The drawings are of people and animals carved into limestone. It was discovered in 1833.

Leo Petroglyths
Admission is FREE

- Open daily dawn to dusk
- Location: near the village of Leo near Jackson, OH
- Phone: 614-297-2630

Some 37 inscriptions in sandstone mark the ancient culture of the Fort Ancient Indians dating between the years 1000 and

1650. The drawings, who's meanings have not yet been translated, are of Indians and animals representing the time and region. Today, visitors can view these creations as well as a scenic ravine, gorge and cliffs.

Lockington Locks
Admission is FREE

- Open daily dawn to dusk
- Location: Lockington, OH
- Phone: 614-297-2630

As part of the Miami and Erie Canal system connecting the Ohio River in Cincinnati to Lake Erie in Toledo, these five stair-step locks were vital to transportation and water supply in the mid nineteenth century. Today, the locks lead to Loramie Creek. The site's remains include the abutments and aqueducts of the locks as well as the dry-lock basin and lockmaster's home.

Ohio Statehouse
Admission is FREE

- Open daily from 7:00 a.m. - 7:00 p.m. (10:00 a.m. - 5:00 p.m. on weekends)
- Location: Downtown Columbus, OH on the corner of High St. and Broad St
- Phone: 614-728-2695

The statehouse is more than a modern day functional meeting place for government officials, it is wrought with historical significance and is one of the oldest working statehouses left in the country. In addition to tours offered to see where and how the state's government officials operate, visitors can enjoy touch-screen kiosks for interactive presentations and view additional educational displays offering much to share about the state's civic milestones and Ohio history.

THE WILD-SIDE OF HISTORY

Naturally, a connection between man and nature, this is where historic events occurred in the company of natural landmarks.

Glacial Grooves
Admission is FREE

- Open daily dawn to dusk
- Location: Kelly's Island in Lake Erie off the Port Clinton, OH shore
- Phone: 419-797-4025

Okay, so this national natural landmark had nothing to do with nature connecting with man as the introduction implies - until man quarried away many other grooves during the 20th century. Today, these 18,000 year-old glacial grooves are "protected" and measure 400 feet long, 35-feet wide and 10-feet deep. Visitors can get up close for a good view and pictures of the grooves from an observation stairway/walkway. There are also marine-fossil remains in the limestone bedrock dating nearly 400 million-years-old.

Logan Elm
Admission is FREE

- Open daily dawn to dusk.
- Location: Route 23 near Circleville, OH
- Phone: 614-297-2630

A plaque now marks the spot where Mingo tribe's Chief Logan delivered a famous speech on Indian and "white-man" relations back in 1774. It was said to have taken place under the shade of a 65-foot tall Elm tree with a trunk measuring 24-feet around. Unfortunately, the tree died in 1964 due to storm damage. The park also has monuments representing other significant Native-Americans and settlers of Ohio.

MOUNDS OF FUN

Well, maybe not "mounds of fun" but certainly mounds of history. The following are ancient burial grounds of various prehistoric Indians throughout Ohio.

Miamisburg Mound
Admission is FREE

• Open daily dawn to dusk
• Location: Mound Avenue in Miamisburg, OH
• Phone: 937-866-4532

Visitors may make the 116 foot climb to the top of this historic mound to capture a panoramic view of the 37-acre park. This burial mound is the largest discovered in Ohio and measures 877 feet around. It was built by the Adena Indians between 800 B.C. and 100 A.D.

Octagonal Earthworks
Admission is FREE

• Open daily dawn to dusk
• Location: Corner of Parkview Road and 33rd Street in Newark, OH
• Phone: 740-344-1919

Built by the Hopwell Indians between 100 B.C. and 500 A.D., this historic complex of burial mounds and earthworks were once one of the most impressive discovered in the U.S. Today, there are still walls adjoining the mounds in the 20-acre circular embankment. Additional smaller mounds are also found opposite the openings within the Octagonal works.

Seip Mound
Admission is FREE

- Open daily dawn to dusk
- Location: Two miles East of Bainbridge, Ohio on Route 50 near Chillicothe, OH
- Phone: 614-297-2630

This is the central burial earthwork in what was once a much larger complex built by the Hopewell Indians between 100 B.C. and 500 A.D. Today, this geometrical archeological discovery measures 240 feet by 130 feet and stands about 30 feet high. Archeologists' discoveries of artifacts buried with the Indians at this site indicate that the Hopwell's were very advanced for their time in developing crafts. The location of addition structures, no longer existent, are outlined with markers to provide visitors with a perspective of what the entire site once looked like.

Shrum Mound
Admission is FREE

- Open daily dawn to dusk
- Location: Campbell Park near the Trabue Road and McKinley Avenue intersection in downtown Columbus, OH
- Phone: 614-297-2630

Built by the Adena Indians approximately 2,000 years ago, it is currently a grass-covered hill 100 foot in diameter and nearly 20 feet high. There are steps leading to the top.

Story Mound
Admission is FREE

- Open daily dawn to dusk
- Location: Near Allen Avenue and Delano Street in northwest Chillicothe, OH

- Phone: 800-686-1535

Story Mound is a prehistoric burial mound dating between 800 B.C. and 100 A.D. It was built by the Adena Indians as a ceremonial place. It is currently nearly 100 feet in diameter and twenty feet high covering almost an acre. It is of note to archeologists because it represents the first documented example of such a structure connected to the Adena's. It was excavated in 1897.

Wright Earthworks
Admission is FREE.

- Open daily dawn to dusk
- Location: Intersection of James St. and Waldo St. in Newark, OH
- Phone: 800-600-7174

These geometrical enclosures were built by the Hopewell Indians between 100 B.C. and 500 A.D. They had religious and social significance to the Indians of the time. The remains measure approximately 50 feet in length. Although city expansion and development has eliminated portions of the Wright Earthworks' original mounds and walls, vital parts of the complex have been preserved.

PARKS

Ohio has sprawling natural beauty from lakes, rivers, forests, swamps and more. Many of the natural treasures are preserved by local, state and national government bodies. Several of the most resourceful parks are featured below but there are so many more throughout Ohio. From state parks to metropolitan parks, there is an abundance of free things to see and do. To find out what activities and sites are available, we encourage you to contact your park(s) of choice and subscribe to their free publication(s) or visit the following Web sites:

- www.ohioparks.net
- www.dnr.state.oh.us/parks/
- www.opraonline.org/
- www.metroparks.net/
- www.clemetparks.com/
- www.metroparkstoledo.com/

Amish Country
Admission is FREE

Plan a visit to see Ohio's "living and working history museum" - the world of the Amish. It is a great day trip to see and learn about the Amish way of life in splendid quality and simplicity. Let's start with the three Ohio counties with significant Amish life bustling within.

- Holmes County: Home to the largest Amish population on the planet. Visit their Web site at www.visitamishcountry.com or go to www.holmescountychamber.com. You may also call 330-674-3975 or 866-OHIO-866.
- Tuscarawas County: Visit www.neotravel.com or call 800-527-3387 for free a brochure.
- Wayne County: Visit www.wooster-wayne.com/wccvb/ or call 800-362-6474.

In addition, free maps, visitors guide and video are available at www.gpubs.com/oac/index.html.

Buckeye Trail
Admission is FREE
- Web Site: www.buckeyetrail.org

Many people fantasize of one day hiking the distance of the

Appalachian Trail. But, did you know that Ohio has its very own version of a marathon hiking exploration awaiting the modern day adventurer? The Buckeye Trail will take its hikers all round Ohio, literally, and expose hikers to all of Ohio's habitats, including that of man. It cuts through urban streets and greenbelt areas, Hocking Hills known to some as the "little Smokies" after the Smokey Mountains, scenic hills and waterfalls, rural waves of amber grain, a towpath along a 19th century canal, a beachhead at Lake Erie and so much more. However, be prepared if you seriously want to tackle this quest, as the entire trail spans 1,300 miles of foot transportation.

The Web site listed above also provides information for shorter excursions covering portions of the Buckeye Trail with day-hikes and featured hikes. It also provides a map of the entire trail and detailed maps of pieces of the trail. The Buckeye Trail is marked with blue blazes on poles and tree trunks so hikers can stay the course.

Hocking Hills
Admission is FREE
- Web Site: www.hockinghillspark.com

This is probably the purest and most beautiful natural landscape in Ohio. In fact, unless you've been there, you wouldn't believe that such a breathtaking place could be found in Ohio. Hocking Hills, located in southeastern Ohio, features extraordinarily picturesque caves, waterfalls, forest, gorges, abundant wildlife, rock outcrops and elevated views. The featured attractions are as follows:

- Old Man's Cave: Most people talk of Hocking Hills and Old Man's Cave synonymously. It is a long stretch of valley that basically has it all. From the rocky cavernous terrain along Old Man's Cave to streams, cliffs, undercut rock, waterfall and plant life.

- Ash Cave: This is an enormous cave-like ridge with an impressive view from the bottom or top - both of which are assessable. It is very high and very wide. People walking along the bottom inner-rim look like ants as you hike toward them along the beautiful gorge. And on a good day, it has water flowing from the cave's peak to a pond floor at the bottom.

- Rock House: No, no music here. Instead, it is basically a cave/cliff with natural window views through the rock. Inside, you may feel like this is a house that could have been used on The Flintstones. It has a spectacular view of the greenery and valley resting far below.

- Cedar Falls: This is a great place to relax and enjoy the rhythm of the pounding water. It has moss-covered cliffs and plenty of natural beauty surrounding the area.

- Cantwell Cliffs: A bit more remote to reach compared to other Hocking Hill's highlights but Cantwell Cliffs is worth it. It's plush forestry, deep valley and narrow passageway along the valley floor will certainly be appreciated by all.

- Conkles Hollow: This area has hiking trails high along the cliffs and along the gorge floor. In any case, it is amidst a refreshing wilderness that seems untouched.

Maumee Bay
Admission is FREE

- Location: 1750 Park Road, #2 · Oregon, OH 43618
- Phone: 419-836-1466
- Web Site: www.maumeebayresort.com

Maumee Bay is Ohio's newest state park and resort. It is a beautiful setting on the shore of Lake Erie and provides a wide-variety of activities for visitors to do for free. Among the beachfront, meadows, woods, wetlands and wildlife, there are hiking and bicycling trails, a nature center with many interactive exhibits, and a wetland boardwalk stretching for miles. In addition, there is an enormous sandy beach on the Lake Erie shore and an inner coastal harbor which features 1,500-foot circular beech. Plus, an outdoor amphitheatre provides evening shows for free throughout the summer. Shows include a variety of musical performances, skits and plays, and magic. Last, there is also fishing and winter activities such as sledding, ice-skating and cross-country skiing available.

NATURE CENTERS

Ohio is certainly blessed with many nature centers. This is a perfect afternoon diversion for nature-lovers, children or those that simply need a quite escape. Although some nature centers charge admission, most do not. It is recommended that you contact your local parks division, visitors bureau or simply check the entertainment section of your local newspaper to find what's available nearby. Although many nature centers appear to be similar, they each have their own distinctive touch. Also, many unique activities occur weekly at these little community jewels - and some are free.

Here are some of the highlights you may find at your nature center:

- Children's playhouses, hollow logs and other fun stuff
- Bird-watching and identification
- Fossils
- Stuffed wildlife
- Real wildlife
- "Wild" exhibits that encourage hands-on exploration
- Historical tools and clothing used by area pioneers
- Reading for pleasure in solitude
- Petting a snake, turtle or reptile

- Gazing at stars and constellations
- Learning the natural history of the area
- Scenic views
- Exhibits of plants, animals and minerals
- Topography maps
- Books and puzzles for visitors to enjoy
- Story-tellers
- Picking a Naturalists brain
- Interactive learning exhibits
- Free publications and maps of hiking trails and activities
- Presentations and other special programs

COVERED BRIDGES

There is just something about a covered bridge that attracts us. It may be the untold history hinted at by its weathered look or the distinct architectural craftsmanship that sets one apart from the other. My goodness, there's even been a feature film about covered bridges. Okay, maybe Bridges of Madison County wasn't exactly about the covered bridges. In any case, Ohio has many covered bridges - most are old and historic and some are new. There are various resources to learn the history of these bridges and where to find them. It makes for a great driving-tour. For more information, visit the following Web sites:

- www.dot.state.oh.us/se/coveredbridges/ - It illustrates a map of Ohio listing each county and the number of covered bridges in it. The county name has a hyperlink to a detailed driving map for the curious to use to go and view the bridges. Note, Ashtabula county in northeast Ohio and Fairfield county in central Ohio top the list with 16 covered bridges each.
- http://www.coveredbridgefestival.org/bridges.htm -

Here, you'll find pictures, details, locations and historical notes about the bridges of Ashtabula county.

- www.visitfairfieldcountyoh.org/coveredbridge.html - Fairfield county's covered bridges are found here with pictures, maps and details regarding each.
- www.members.aol.com/jreinhl/tours/tour-ndx.htm - Provides detailed directions and touring information for covered bridges found all over the state.

LIGHTHOUSES

Much like a covered bridge, lighthouses have a certain appeal that people just love to look at. Some people even collect lighthouse miniatures or lawn ornaments without ever having been inside one. One of the best source regarding our state's lighthouses is at http://www.unc.edu/~rowlett/lighthouse/oh.htm. It provides information about each lighthouse, including where to find it, historical and other interesting facts, as well as very nice photographs. Please note that some lighthouses are no longer actively operating. Also, many charge for tours of their interior. However, you can't be charged for an outdoor view.

HOW'D THEY DO THAT?
(Interesting Tours)

There are so many things we take for granted or to which we never give much thought. Often times, we never stop to think, "How did they do that?"

If you are genuinely curious by nature or just enjoy the behind-the-scenes look at things, the tours ahead are ideal for you.

The free tours highlighted in this section are entertaining as much as they are educational. You can observe how dolls, crayons, pasta, popcorn, glass and crystal, baskets and candy are manufactured. However, not all of these tours are about making something. Some provide an insiders view of the beautiful interior of historic theatres, including the backstage areas. And others show the operations of historic gristmills or the architecture of a 19th Century mall.

Find the tours that interest you and go find out how they do that.

ANTHONY THOMAS CANDY COMPANY
Admission is FREE

- Open by appointment Mondays through Fridays 10:00 a.m. - 3:00 p.m.
- Location: 1777 Arling Gate Lane · Columbus, OH 43228
- Phone: 614-272-9221 or 614-274-8405
- Web Site: www.anthony-thomas.com/tour/index.html

Have you ever fantasized about visiting Willy Wonka and the Chocolate Factory? Well, in about an hour's time, you can almost taste it. Visitors can walk along a glass-enclosed suspended catwalk to see candy made at this 152,000 square-foot state-of-the-art candy factory. In one shift, 25,000 pounds of chocolate are produced. Even Augustus Loof would be left satisfied (sorry, no chocolate river here).

BEAR'S MILL
Admission is FREE

- Call for hours
- Location: 6450 Arcanum-Bear's Mill Road · Greenville, OH 45331
- Phone: 937-548-5112

Come, mill around on a self-guided tour of all four stories of this 1849 grist mill. Surprisingly, it is still operating more than 150 years after being built. The mill is powered by water and is used to produce flours and pancake mixes. The weathered exterior and rustic interior makes for a good picture. And inside, there is a store on the main level and handmade pottery created by the Bear's Mill potters.

BIG BEAR WAREHOUSE
Admission is FREE

- Open by appointment on Tuesdays and Wednesdays
- Location: 770 W. Goodale Blvd. · Columbus, OH 43212
- Phone: 614-464-6750

This eclectic tour will treat you to a view of train cars being unloaded, a -brrrrr- walk into a freezer and a stroll through a room used to ripen bananas.

BOYD'S CRYSTAL ART GLASS
Admission is FREE

- Open Mondays through Fridays from 7:00 a.m. - 3:30 p.m.
- Location: 1203 Morton Ave. · Cambridge, OH 43725
- Phone: 740-439-2077
- Web Site: www.boydglass.com

The people at Boyd's offer an open invitation for anyone to stop by and see glassmaking up close. Boyd's is a family operated business that produce several hundred glass pieces daily, including many collectible figurines and ornamental pieces.

CARNATION BASKET COMPANY
Admission is FREE

- Call for hours
- Location: 112 Prospect Ave. · Alliance, OH 44601
- Phone: 800-823-7231 or 330-823-7231
- Web Site: www.basketsplusmore.com

This small-family owned and operated basket company produces maple baskets sold nationwide. During tours, you can even talk to weavers while you see baskets made by hand literally from bottom to top.

CLIFTON MILL & GORGE
Admission is FREE

- Open various times. It is recommended to call ahead before visiting
- Location: Clifton, OH
- Phone: 937-767-5501
- Web Site: www.cliftonmill.com

Built two hundred years ago in 1802, this is still one of the largest water-powered gristmills still around in the U.S. Visitors can tour all five floors of the mill and learn how it operated and what took place on each floor. In addition, a scenic hike is accessible nearby and provides panoramic views of the Little Miami River and overlooks to the gorge.

CREEGAN COMPANY
Admission is FREE

- Open Mondays through Saturdays from 10:00 a.m. - 4:00 p.m. (Closes at 2:00 p.m. on Saturdays)
- Location: 510 Washington St. · Steubenville, OH 43952
- Phone: 740-283-3708
- Web Site: www.creegans.com

See the magic of the world of animation at the nation's largest manufacturer of animated and costumed characters at this small town family-owned factory. One of their elite list of clientele includes Walt Disney so not only are they big, but they are good. See them at their craft up close and personal as they design, sculpt and decorate animated creatures of all kinds. You can even see the "guts" of electronic figures and see how they work. Don't be alarmed if you see body parts strewn about the place on your tour - it's not real, or is it?

CRYSTAL TRADITIONS
Admission is FREE

- Open Mondays through Fridays from 10:00 a.m. - 5:00 p.m.
- Location: 145 Madison St. · Tiffin, OH 44883
- Phone: 419-448-4286
- Web Site: www.crystaltraditions.com

It's fascinating to see the art of glass blowing as a molten blob is transformed into fine art before your very eyes. This tour demonstrates glass blowing and hand cutting of crystal into a beautiful pieces to display. During the time there, visitors will hear tales of glass making from its ancient roots through to the modern age. Enjoy!

DIXON TICONDEROGA (PRANG) CRAYON FACTORY
Admission is FREE

- Open by appointment only
- Location: Sandusky, OH
- Phone: 419-625-9545

Do you want to know who's responsible for that pesky "Yellow #2 Pencil?" Not only will this tour tell you all you ever needed to know and more about this mysteriously popular lead writing instrument, it'll demonstrate how crayons are made. Yep, from mixing colors, pouring molds, cooling, labeling and packaging, you will become a crayon expert.

163

GARRETTS MILL
Admission is FREE

- Open Mondays through Thursdays from 11:00 a.m. - 10:00 p.m.; Saturdays from 11:00 a.m. - 11:00 p.m. (Closed Saturdays between 2:00 p.m. and 4:00 p.m. and open Sundays from 11:00 a.m. - 4:00 p.m.)
- Location: 8148 Main Street · Garrettsville, OH 44231
- Phone: 330-527-5849

This historic building was built in 1804 and still operates as a gristmill, restaurant and micro-brewery. See grain ground to flour by 3,000-pound millstones, move to different floors via conveyer belt and finally sifted and bagged.

HARVEYSBURG FREE BLACK SCHOOL
Admission is FREE

- Open by appointment only
- Location: Harveysburg, OH 45032
- Phone: 513-897-6195
- Web Site: http://www.shakerwssg.org/first_black_school_in_the_united.htm

Welcome to the very first free school in Ohio for black (African-American) children. The town was once a renowned stop along the Underground Railroad. The one-room schoolhouse was founded in the 1830's by the Quakers and was recently restored to reflect its former self as a nineteenth-century classroom. In addition to providing education to young freed slaves, the school also taught to Native-American children in the area.

ISAAC LUDWIG MILL
Admission is FREE

- Open May through October on Wednesdays through Sundays from 10:00 a.m. - 5:00 p.m.
- Location: Grand Rapids, OH
- Phone: 419-535-3050

Some people just love the smell of sawdust. Well, if you're one of these people, try visiting this restored and working 19th century saw and gristmill. Visitors will learn about the milling process and can see how the mill is powered by a neighboring canal.

JONES' POTATO CHIPS
Admission is FREE

- Open Mondays through Fridays from 9:00 a.m. - 1:00 p.m. (tours by appointment only)
- Location: 265 Bowman St. · Mansfield, OH
- Phone: 419-529-9424
- Web Site: www.joneschips.com

Some like it hot - or warm at least. Potato chips that is! If you were every curious about how chips were made, this is the right place to be. This 40-minute tour demonstrates the entire process and at the end, you get to sample a chip right off of the production line. That's right, take a potato at one end and see it transform into a potato chip bagged and ready for distribution by the time you get to the other end.

JUNGLE JIM'S INTERNATIONAL
FARMERS MARKET
Self-guided tour is FREE
(Formal basic group tours cost $1 per person)

- Open Mondays through Thursdays all day (8:00 a.m. - 10:00 p.m.) and Friday mornings

165

- Location: 5440 Dixie Hwy · Fairfield, OH 45014
- Phone: 513-674-6023
- Web Site: www.junglejims.com

This is grocery shopping like you've never seen before! To browse the isles at Jungle Jim's is quiet an experience. Foods from around the world are everywhere you turn, as well as jaw dropping scenery. The attractions include the following:

- The Jungle Scene complete with waterfall and wildlife
- The General Mills Big G Cereal Bowl Band perched on the S.S. Minnow
- Singing Creatures
- The Brain (a pesky know-it-all employee)
- The Giant Mushroom rising above the one-acre produce department
- European gourmet village
- The Cake Canopy, International Elephant Gates and more

KING'S GLASS ENGRAVING
Admission is FREE

- Call for hours
- Location: 181 S. Washington St. · Tiffin, OH 44883
- Phone: 419-447-0232
- Web Site: www.kingsglassinc.com

Daily demonstrations of glass engraving are made available to visitors. Engraved glass includes fluted champagne glasses, crystal bells and more.

LEE MIDDLETON ORIGINAL DOLLS
Admission is FREE

- Call to make advanced registration for tour

- Location: 1301 Washington Blvd. · Belpre, OH 45714
- Phone: 740-423-1481 or 800-233-7479
- Web Site: www.leemiddleton.com

Tour a living interactive dollhouse (The largest doll factory in the U.S.). And see how they are made to look and feel lifelike. Not only that but visit the Newborn Nursery where you can actually adopt one of the baby dolls. Doll collectors and just the curious descend on this factory annually by the thousands. The problem is, if you bring your daughter, she may never want to leave.

LONGABERGER MUSEUM AND FACTORY
Admission is FREE

- Call for hours
- Location: 5563 Raiders Road · Frazeysburg, OH 43822
- Phone: 740-322-5588
- Web Site: www.longaberger.com

Longaberger headquarters is inside the world's largest basket as the entire building's architecture is shaped like a giant basket including the handles. A visit to the Homestead will treat everyone to a comprehensive gallery, plant tours and basket-making demonstrations. There is also a theatre where visitors can view the history of the Longaberger company. One of the more interesting aspects of the museum and tour is the Mezzanine where guests can gaze down at the 250,000 square-foot weaving floor and get a bird's-eye-view of the activity below.

MIDDLEFIELD CHEESE HOUSE
Admission is FREE

- Open Mondays through Saturdays from 8:00 a.m. - 5:30 p.m.

- Location: 15815 Nauvoo Rd. · Middlefield, OH 44062
- Phone: 800-327-9477
- Web Site: www.middlefieldcheese.com

Who stole my cheese? Located in the fourth largest Amish community in the country, the Middlefield Cheese House has been serving award winning Swiss cheese for several generations. Visitors will learn what's involved in the cheese-making process and see cheese carvings, antique cheese production equipment and more. Don't forget to sample the cheese before you leave.

MIEIR'S WINE CELLARS
Admission is FREE

- Open for scheduled tours from June 1st through October 31st and by appointment only from November through May
- Location: 6955 Plainfield Rd. · Cincinnati, OH
- Phone: 513-891-2900 or 800-346-2941
- Web Site: www.mieirswinecellars.com

This is the oldest and largest winery in the state dating back more than 100 years. There's something about a winery that just makes you want to do a little taste-testing of the finished product after meandering through century-old wine cellars.

MOSSER GLASS
Admission is FREE

- Open Mondays through Fridays from 8:30 a.m. - 10:30 a.m. and 12:30 p.m. - 3:00 p.m.
- Location: 9279 Cadiz Road · Cambridge, OH 43725
- Phone: 740-439-1827

- Web Site: www.mosserglass.com

Learn about the glass-making business while visiting and touring the facilities at Glosser Glass. The tour begins where glass-making does - with sand. And then goes on to include other steps in the process such as heating the ingredients at 2,500 degrees Fahrenheit. The finished products include just about anything from water pitchers to ashtrays.

MURPHY'S LIGHTHOUSES
Admission is FREE

- Open Mondays through Saturdays from 8:00 a.m. - 5:00 p.m.
- Location: 2017 W. Sylvania Ave. · Toledo, OH 43613
- Phone: 419-480-9999 or 800-288-0563
- Web Site: http://lighthousesbymurphy.com/

Making models is one thing but the making of Murphy's lighthouses is in a league of its own. Terry "Murphy" Murray doesn't just make model and garden lighthouses, he researches down to the last detail, every intricacy of the original for which the replica is modeled. This includes a personal visit to the real lighthouse. He's been at it for 40 years and has amassed quiet a following, including the world of the rich and famous - i.e. the late Katherine Hepburn. Come - watch the master at work.

OHIO AGRICULTURAL RESEARCH AND DEVELOPMENT CENTER
Admission is FREE

- Call for hours
- Location: Wooster, OH (Ohio State University)
- Phone: 330-202-3503
- Web Site: http://www.oardc.ohio-state.edu/visitor/

169

If you want a beautiful place to relax and take in the surroundings - visit the 85-acre Secrest Arboretum. Then, continue onto the greenhouse conservatory and complete a very fulfilling guided-tour with a visit to the historical museum on site. The purpose of the OARDC is to research food, agriculture, family and environment and produce safe and healthy food and agricultural products.

OLD STONE CHURCH
Admission is FREE

- Open Mondays and Thursdays from 11:30 a.m. - 1:30 p.m.
- Location: 91 Public Square · Cleveland, OH
- Phone: 216-241-6145

If walls could talk, the sandstone of this Romanesque style church would have about 150 years of history to share. If you like beautiful architecture, take a self-guided tour of this house of worship. It is peculiarly set in a corner of Cleveland's public square with neighboring skyscrapers all around.

OLD WOMAN CREEK NATIONAL ESTUARINE RESEARCH RESERVE
Admission is FREE

- Call for hours
- Location: Erie County near Huron, OH
- Phone: 419-433-4601
- Web Site:http://www.ocrm.nos.noaa.gov/nerr/ reserves/nerroldwoman.html

This is a thoroughly educational opportunity to learn about the precious ecosystems that surround us. This is the smallest reserve in the National Estuarine Research System but the only Great Lakes-type freshwater estuary in the system. It provides multimedia presentations, interpretive field trips, guided-tours and a visitor center with natural history exhibits and a library. The reserve features freshwater marshes, swamp forests, a barrier beach, upland forest, estuarine waters, stream and the nearby Lake Erie shore.

PLAYHOUSE SQUARE CENTER
Admission is FREE

- Open usually on the first weekend of the month between 10:00 a.m. and 11:30 a.m.
- Location: State Theater · 1519 Euclid Avenue · Cleveland, OH 44115
- Phone: 216-771-4444
- Web Site: http://www.playhousesquare.com/tours/index.cfm

Did you ever think you could actually go to the theater and get backstage passes in casual clothes for free? Well, you can if you tour the historic Allen, Ohio, State and Palace theaters. The Playhouse Square theater district is the largest performing arts complex in the United States except for New York City. And it attracts more than 1 million people annually. After nearly being forgotten and destroyed, the theaters were reclaimed in the largest theater restoration project in the world. Today, they are radiant and provide for a very worthwhile visit. The tour takes about an hour and a half and includes the lobbies, lavish auditoriums and backstage areas.

POPCORN GALLERY
Admission is FREE

- Call for appointment
- Location: Lima, OH
- Phone: 419-227-2676

Yah, yah - to make popcorn you merely need to "nuke" it on high for four minutes. But how do you really "make" popcorn, let alone some 40 different flavors? Exactly what makes the kernels "pop?" Well, find out by popping over to see the entire popping and flavor mixing process. Last question. Just how did Native-Americans come up with more than 700 varieties of popcorn? Take the tour and find out.

QUAKER SQUARE
Admission is FREE

- Call for hours
- Location: 135 South Broadway · Akron, OH 44308
- Phone: 330-253-5970
- Web Site: www.quakersquare.com

What was once the original Quaker Oats Company is now home to a unique-looking retail complex providing shopping, restaurants, hotel and entertainment center. The buildings, known as silos, are unique and listed in the National Register of Historic Places. The company's rich history is told with historic advertising memorabilia and includes accounts of how Ferdinand Schumacher originally attempted to sell his breakfast oats, as well as how a fire nearly destroyed everything.

ROBINSON RANSBOTTOM POTTERY COMPANY
Admission is FREE

- Open Mondays through Fridays (Call for hours)
- Location: Roseville, OH 43777
- Phone: 740-697-7355
- Web Site: www.ransbottompottery.com

Don't expect any ghosts guiding these professionals at the pottery-wheel. This century-old family business creates stoneware pottery for the lawn, garden and home. On the tour, visitors will see how raw clay is transformed to a finished product of art. Along the way, there are stops to watch each stage of the process. It includes grinding, decorating, clay pressing, various kilns, a warehouse and more.

ROSSI PASTA
Admission is FREE

- Open Mondays through Fridays (Call for hours)
- Location: Marietta, OH 45750
- Phone: 800-227-6774
- Web Site: www.rossipasta.com

It's AMORA! Fall in love with Rossi Pasta on a tour that's sure to make your mouth water. They've been creating pasta and sauces in northern Italian tradition since 1981. Visitors are treated to a tour demonstrating the complete process that goes into making 19 flavors of Rossi Pasta.

THE ARCADE
Admission is FREE

- Open Mondays through Saturdays from 7:00 a.m. - 7:00 p.m.
- Location: 401 Euclid Avenue · Cleveland, OH

This 1890 structure was the first building in Cleveland to be placed on the National Register of Historic Places. It is a site to see. Inside, it features a 5-story atrium loaded with ornate brass décor and gargoyles perched high above. The iron and glass skylight allows for the sun to splash in on the bustling little shops that still operate in this urban landmark.

THE WEST SIDE MARKET
Admission is FREE

- Open Mondays and Wednesdays from 7:00 a.m. - 4:00 p.m. and Fridays and Saturdays from 7:00 a.m. - 6:00 p.m.
- Location: The corner of West 25th and Lorain in Cleveland's Ohio City Neighborhood
- Phone: 216-664-3386
- Web Site: www.westsidemarket.com

Take a self-guided tour of this 1912 multi-cultural historical landmark. It is produce shopping old-world style and features more than 100 ethnic vendors selling first-rate vegetables, meats, fresh-fish, pastries and a lot more. There is a viewing area high above the main-market floor, which provides tourists with a birds-eye view of the hustle and bustle going on below. Tours of the market's underground are available by request.

ACTION-REACTION
(Your Own Fun-Filled Ideas)

Jump-start your brain and think of some alternative fun and
recreational ideas to entertain your family and friends -
for free.

If you take action, there is sure to be a reaction. And this is
the stuff that memories are made to last a lifetime. The section
ahead lists ideas to get the creative juices flowing. Although
some may seem like common sense, they are not common
practice.

Now, take action and prepare for the reaction - fun.

With a little creativity you can come up with some great ideas for your own free entertainment and recreation. In order to get you started, consider the list of options at your disposal below. There is something fun to do to fill nearly a month of your calendar. Much of the following requires merely picking up the phone once and asking for a tour, if that.

- **Airport tour**: Whether you can arrange a private tour or just go with the kids to watch airplanes come and go, it is something out of the ordinary that you can do for free.

- **Animal shelter**: Kind of a sad visit if you don't plan to adopt an animal but you may consider volunteering to walk a dog. Sometimes, the facility will allow you to tour its clinic and explain the shots and other treatments. It's good for kids to learn about pet care.

- **Antique store**: Treat it like it's a historical museum and just browse the unique items that were once commonplace in homes generations ago. If you have a question about the origins of something, ask. Other considerations along the same line are auctions, flea-markets and garage sales to some extent.

- **Bank**: Call up your local bank and ask for a tour. Winter Advisory: If you wear a ski-mask, take it off before entering the bank. Kids love the big vaults.

- **Beach**: Whether you live near the Lake Erie shore or an inner Ohio lake, you need to spend at least one day at the beach. With kids or without, build a sand castle or just go swimming. For those who've never been to the ocean or a Great Lake, head up to the Erie shore and take a stroll along one of its many sprawling beaches.

- **Community events**: Many communities have a gazebo, town square or some other place that offers summertime concerts, plays or magic shows for free. Go.

- **Camping**: To do this for free, just set up a tent in the backyard and roast hotdogs and marshmallows. Afterward, tell stories. If you have "cabin-fever" during the winter, go camping in the basement or living room. It's fun to actually do something a bit unconventional once in a while.

- **Courtroom**: Not the place to practice heckling but you may want to have a little fun testing your artistic talent by drawing a picture of the judge, prosecutor or defendant. Hey, if television shows like Judge Judy or People's Court attract such an audience, why not see the action live.

- **Driving tours**: Have you ever taken a "Sunday after noon drive?" Relax and explore the road less traveled. Head down an old country road or state route until you hit half a tank of gas, stop, have a picnic and then go home. You may want to randomly pick a place on the Ohio map and just go for the sake of going. Another idea is to visit a small town downtown that looks like something out of a Norman Rockwell painting. For starters, go to little Ohio towns like Greenville, Delaware, Lebanon, Bryan or Chagrin Falls.

- **Fire stations and police stations**: Just call the nearest one and ask for a visit. I'd be surprised if they didn't roll out the red carpet for the kids and give them a tour they won't forget. Make sure to bring a camera as many excellent photo-ops await.

- **Fireworks**: Ooooowww-Ahhhhhhhhh. Need I say more. Well, yes. You know the kid in you died when you stop going to the fireworks show on the Fourth-of-July.

- **Fishing**: Yah, I know, you have to buy a fishing license therefore it is not free. Technically, yes. But try this. Tie a string to a stick, grab a bucket, some munchies and other things you'd take on a fishing trip and cast away off your porch or deck with the kids and use your imagination.

- **Hiking-biking and walking**: Find a trail, a park or somewhere scenic and rejuvenate yourself. If you've never walked in the summer rain - what are you waiting for? (Rain-advisory - be sure it isn't an electrical storm!)

- **Hospital**: Again, just call and ask for a tour. Think of the eye-opening fun the kids could have or even the learning experience you might have.

- **Ice skating**: You may look like Bambi learning to walk if you haven't gone for a while but oh what fun you'll have. Whether it's with a significant other or the kids, plan to do it at least once this winter.

- **Library or bookstore**: Find out what events take place and when. Many are free such as story-time at the library where a storyteller entertains the children with excellent tales. Also, rediscover everything else that's free at your local library like videos, DVDs, CDs, CD-ROMs, magazines, newspapers and hmmm, what am I forgetting? Oh yah - books!

- **Model homes**: Create your own home and garden show. Just go to dream or get ideas for your own home improvement or landscaping project. Bring a camera.

- **Newspaper**: If your local paper is nice enough to give you a tour of their operation I dare you to yell - "stop the press!"

- **Parades**: Every town has them. Isn't it time you go to one? Ohio's major cities have elaborate parades on holidays like Thanksgiving, St. Patrick's Day and others.

- **Picnic-in-the-Park**: This is not done enough by most people anymore. To enhance the experience, make your own kite ala The Little Rascals and see if you can get it to fly. Another idea for a trip to the park is to bring some bread to feed the ducks. And if you and your spouse need to rekindle the flame - try walking barefoot-in-the-park.

- **Post-office**: This could be an interesting learning experience for kids. Call your local post-office and ask for a look see.

- **Radio or television station**: Just another tour option that most stations are happy to provide the listening or viewing public. In our modern-day society, this could prove to be a fascinating event for the grown-ups too.

- **Restaurant**: Find a unique restaurant or see a series of different ethnic places to see how interesting cuisines are prepared and what goes on behind the scenes. Most places love to show-off their businesses.

- **Sledding**: Always a fun thing to do to get out of the house in the winter at any age.

- **Sunrise Sunset**: Seeing it is something everyone should do at least once a year. Come on, we can all fit that into our busy schedules.

- **Vineyards**: Most will treat you to a free tour of the winery and explain the behind-the-scenes operation. If you're lucky - and of age - you may even be treated to a little taste-test of their finished product.

- **Water Plant/power plant**: Yet another tour awaiting your phone call.

If all else fails, open your local paper and see what special events are planned for free. You may also contact the Visitors Bureau at the state, county and local levels and request a free brochure or newsletter that keeps you abreast of the options available year-round. A thorough list of Visitors Bureaus across the state can be found at http://www.ohiotourism.com/visitor/local_tour_org.asp.

INDEX
(Alphabetical)

185

INDEX
(Geographical)

190

ABOUT THE AUTHOR

Frank Satullo is a 34-year-old marketing-communications professional living in Strongsville, Ohio with his wife Rebecca (Native of Greenville, Ohio), daughter Cara and son Dominic. Frank is a native of Avon Lake, Ohio).

Frank created and currently operates a Web site: OhioTraveler.com - a family fun-site. He earned a Bachelor of Arts degree at the University of Toledo and served in the U.S. Army as a satellite communications specialist stationed in Europe.

The Satullo's enjoy being part of a large family that reside throughout the Cleveland, Columbus, Cincinnati, Akron and Dayton areas. For recreation, they enjoy the outdoors and frequently hike, bike, swim, canoe and camp all over the state.